M000083937

When
to Say

When to Say

Yes

The 5 Steps
to Protect
Your Time

DON KHOURI, PhD

PAGE TWO

Copyright © 2021 by Don Khouri, PhD

All rights reserved. No part of this book may be reproduced, stored in a retrieval system or transmitted, in any form or by any means, without the prior written consent of the publisher, except in the case of brief quotations, embodied in reviews and articles. Some names and identifying details have been changed to protect the privacy of individuals.

ISBN 978-1-77458-139-1 (paperback)
ISBN 978-1-77458-140-7 (ebook)

Page Two
pagetwo.com

Edited by Lesley Erickson
Copyedited by Jenny Govier
Cover and interior design by Setareh Ashrafologhalai

whentosayyes.com

Contents

Introduction
The Missing Link in
Productivity Systems

DO WE TRULY need another book on productivity? Well, if the number of people who tell me they're busy when I ask them how they are is any indication, we do. Busy is the new default, but it doesn't have to be.

If you are reading this book, you may be looking for an extra edge to make you more productive. Or maybe you purchased the book because you are overwhelmed by requests for your time, and you are not sure how to respond. Maybe you are looking for more balance in your work and home life. Maybe you want to figure out how to deal with your never-ending to-do list. You have likely tried many other productivity systems before and found that some work, some don't. Maybe you feel like there's still something missing in your system.

I wrote this book for those who struggle with too much to do and who believe they don't have enough time to do it. I've been reading productivity books and studying productivity for thirty years, and what I have learned in my quest to understand the secrets of the most productive people is that there is a missing link in current productivity systems. The authors tell people how to manage their projects or to-do lists, but they don't discuss the fact that to-do lists on their own don't work. Why don't they work? Because our brains are hardwired to get in the way of being productive, and the result is that we're constantly busy rather than purposely productive.

Existing productivity tools and advice either help us manage what is already on our list or help us organize the list in a way that helps us execute it. We need a system to determine what gets put on our plate in the first place. As the title of this book suggests, the missing link in productivity systems is knowing when to say yes.

In his book *When,* Dan Pink discusses the secrets of perfect timing. He uses research from psychology, biology, and economics to explain the best time to do certain things like switch careers or quit a job. He forecasts a new trend toward when-to books rather than how-to books. In this book, you'll learn when to say yes to requests for your time—and when to say no.

My personal quest to understand the mindset of the most productive people unknowingly began in 1989, when I took a two-day personal productivity seminar called "Managing Actions and Projects" (MAP) delivered by guru David Allen. I swaggered out on the final day feeling enthusiastic, joyful, and excited, as if I could accomplish anything and there was nothing standing in my way. A colleague of mine had recommended the seminar early in my software-development career, and it fueled my hunger for performance improvement. During the seminar, I learned some of the important basic ideas of personal productivity, such as how to manage a calendar, how to create action lists, and how to organize a reference system.

After the seminar finished on Friday afternoon, I went back to my cubicle and stayed late so I could implement everything I had learned. First, I tackled the piles of paper on my desk. Each pile had a purpose, and within each pile were buried incomplete tasks and unresolved commitments. With each scrap of paper, I made a decision on the next action required, where to file it, or whether to trash it. I labeled every file folder, sorted them alphabetically, and stored them neatly in my file drawer.

I set up three stacking letter trays—the top one for inbox, the middle one for pending, and the bottom for filing. I created one place to document all my projects and commitments.

When I was finished, there was nothing on my desk except for my computer, my stacking trays, and a picture of my car. I sprayed it and scrubbed it all down. I left four hours later with a clear mind and an empty plate, feeling completely current and ready to conquer the world. Clear desk, clear mind.

What I learned in MAP served me well in my corporate career and allowed me to advance to senior technology positions. The skills enabled me to remain calm in the midst of a crisis. The ability to know what's important, what must be done today, and what can be deferred in the moment is critical. If we are trying to manage emergencies at the same time we're thinking about responding to Bill and calling Amy, our attention will be diverted.

When I worked at Fidelity Investments between 1987 and 2008, there was a culture of figuring out how to do it, whatever it was. As a software solutions provider, my teams knew it was never acceptable to tell our customers, "No, we can't do it." Rather, it was a discussion about priorities, or a tradeoff between time and other factors. So, the more appropriate response was, "We can do that, and we will need more time," or, "We can do that instead of feature *x*." A good software project manager will prioritize time, quality, cost, and functionality as part of the project charter. When you take this approach with your business customers, you create an environment that opens up dialogue, builds credibility, and fosters strong partnerships.

In addition to what I learned in the corporate world, I continued to ask myself: What makes some people more productive than others? Seeking a clear answer, I decided to pursue a PhD in human and organizational systems with a focus on personal productivity. Okay, you've got to admit, that's pretty geeky. I'm not finding the answers I want, so I go spend five years of my life becoming a PhD. A bit overboard maybe. However, I enjoyed this journey for a number of reasons: It was challenging and fulfilling, and I connected with amazing people I call friends today. And it's where I learned that it is not at all about the goal; it is about who you become in achieving the goal.

I also learned this lesson from talking directly with highly productive people. I wanted to understand their mindset, so I interviewed chief information officers (CIOs) and chief technology officers (CTOs) around the United States and asked them how they evaluated requests for their time. CIOs and CTOs have the most senior technology roles in organizations. One doesn't get to be the most senior tech person without some level of self-management and focus on productivity. They are highly successful by at least one measure (career), and that's certainly not the only measure. Each of them spent ninety minutes total completing a one-on-one interview with me and a trusted self-assessment that addresses goal setting, priorities, planning, scheduling, time management, and organization. During the interviews, and as I analyzed the transcripts after, I investigated how participants experienced requests for their time. I asked questions like the following:

- What type of requests are made of you?
- How do you manage these requests?
- What was your thought process when saying no?
- How did you process two requests that were both critical?
- Describe a situation where you had no choice but to say yes.

What is encouraging is that the empirical data from the self-assessment supported the qualitative data from the interviews.

It was through these interviews, and as an executive coach and entrepreneur leading a team of coaches, that I discovered the missing link. I heard clearly from midlevel executives that they have difficulty saying no, and I think this is true of many people. In fact, leaders prefer not to say no. They associate more pain with saying no today than they do with the potential pain of having too much to do later. "I very seldom say no, because 'no' just upsets people and puts them on the defensive," one exclaimed. "It is hard for me to say no; I would rather figure out how to do something," said another. "One thing I never think about is, do I have permission to say no? I'd rather figure out how to do something," said yet another.

The problem is that if we say yes to everything, we end up with too much on our plate, with endless to-do lists and fruitless attempts at multitasking to get it all done. We get stuck in the busy trap. Instead, we need to know when to say yes and when to say no. We need a system to triage incoming requests.

It's that simple. If we successfully triage requests, we stop bleeding time.

In my own life, I developed a simple five-step practice that could be applied to all requests for my time, including requests from bosses, colleagues, friends, family, and even myself. And now I'm sharing these steps with you. The Five Steps to Protect Your Time are as follows:

1   Create your roadmap.
2   Define your relationship hierarchy.
3   Assess the quality of the request.
4   Prioritize and reprioritize.
5   Master delegation.

Each step is accompanied by a simple question that you'll ask yourself each time you make a decision.

1
Does it align with
my roadmap?

2
Who is
asking?

3
Is it a quality
request?

4
Where does it fit on
my priority list?

5
To whom can
I delegate?

Now, this may seem like a lot of steps simply to decide when to say yes. You may be thinking, *This is just way too complex. The world is moving too fast to be able to consider all of these when evaluating a single request for my time.* I get it. There is a lot to consider. My promise is that with only a bit of practice you'll quickly get to the point where following the Five Steps will be instinctive. Granted, it will take some work to get there. You're reading this book because you are already successful, and I know that didn't come without some elbow grease. The things you do instinctively today may have been out of reach for you before.

This book is not about time management, which Alec Mackenzie and Pat Nickerson defined in their book, *The Time Trap,* as a process by which an individual can more effectively accomplish a goal or a task. I'd like to redefine time management as "taking control by consciously evaluating requests for your time." When we have a system that tells us when to say yes, then we are managing time. It's as simple as that.

What I offer is a better version of SMART goals, a better way to schedule your time, a new way to look at your collective projects, and a new way to think about what's important in your life. It's my commitment to *kaizen.* This is a Japanese word actually made of two words. *Kai* means "change," and *zen* means "better." *Kaizen* is about making small, incremental changes every day. What I share in this book is a way to transform being busy into being purposefully productive. This knowledge will give you back a sense of control over your time and your results.

Have you ever heard the expression, "If you want something done, give it to a busy person?" It's a true statement, but not for the reasons you're thinking. The expression came about because there was a belief that the busy person is more productive. That is actually not true. What's happening is that busy people say yes to everything. They work longer hours to get it all done, and as a result they are likely saying no to things subconsciously (family, health, planning, personal development) that they don't intend to set aside.

So, let's get purposely productive.

In what follows, I'll lead you through each step of the process using examples and exercises, and I hope you will love it. But first you'll need to change your mindset. Part One will help you understand the distinction between being busy and being purposely productive. It will convince you to think differently about the to-do list, to stop trying to multitask, and to recognize the perfectly human cognitive biases and limitations that prevent all of us from making well-thought-out, deliberative decisions. Part Two takes you through the Five Steps in detail, and Part Three shows you how to integrate these steps into a cohesive system and apply it to one of the biggest drains on our time—email. Throughout it all, you'll learn to think and talk differently about work and life. I encourage you to be productive, not busy; to process your email rather than check it; to invest your time rather than "spend" it.

To get the most of this book and my system, I recommend reading the book from beginning to end without skipping the exercises in the Productivity Corners. They'll help you implement the concepts and systems in this book and make them real. They'll provide you with a productivity toolkit that will set you up for work and life. Do the exercises in the order they appear, and don't be tempted to skip ahead.

I've summarized many of these tools in the Appendix so you have a helpful reference when you need them in future.

My aunt Millie makes the best cinnamon twists in the world. When I was a kid, I loved them, and because she knew I loved them so much, she would always leave some aside for me to take home when I visited her. The ingredients are flour, margarine, sour cream, walnuts, sugar, and cinnamon. The recipe is simple. You mix the flour, margarine, and sour cream together, separate it into four balls, and refrigerate overnight. The next day you take the cinnamon and sugar and mix it in with the dough, pat the dough into a flattened circle, and put chopped walnuts on the edge. Cut the dough into eight pieces like a pie, and roll each piece from the edge to the middle. Brush each twist with milk and sprinkle cinnamon and sugar on top. Bake on the rack above the middle rack at 375 degrees Fahrenheit for twenty-five minutes or until golden brown.

That's it. I didn't say healthy, I said simple. Now, she has shared the recipe with many, many people, including some great cooks I know. And the twists never come out the same.

One person decided that cooking on the middle shelf would work better, but it didn't. Someone else said she bakes everything at 350 degrees, not 375 degrees. That didn't work either. Someone else decided to use dates along the edge instead of walnuts. Good, but different, and not Aunty Millie's cinnamon twists.

I joked with her, when I asked her to share the recipe, that I would make them vegan with vegan sour cream, almond milk, and a replacement for margarine.

Half joking and half annoyed, she said, "No, no. Either make them this way or don't make them at all."

My point is this: All along the way, the others changed something in the recipe and wondered why it didn't come out the same. During your journey into practicing the Five Steps to Protect Your Time, you will be tempted to cut something out and try something different. Trust the process. I know it works.

PART ONE

Change Your Mindset

Your busyness doesn't mean you're being effective. Effectiveness is about the "what," not the "how much."

TAL GUR

Break Out of the Busy Trap

'M BUSY!

I'm crazy busy!

I'm scary busy!

These are typical answers I get to the question, "How are you?" Everyone is busy these days. "Busy" sometimes can even be a badge of honor.

People actually assume I'm busy. It happens often. For example, I received this email from a coaching company:

> I know you are *extremely* busy, but I'm following up to see if you'd be open to booking a call with one of our consultants...
> so they may "wow!" you (as per our previous conversation :)).

This message caught my attention, so I asked the sender, "Curious though, what makes you think or know that I am extremely busy?"

She was polite enough to respond with, "I am going by my experience with calling hundreds of highly successful entrepreneurs per week (I've been doing this for more than ten years), and their feedback."

And another email message: "Occasionally, people aren't able to fully take advantage of their free fourteen-day trial of [fill in your favorite company]. We get it... you're busy!" This one was interesting because it was not addressed to me personally:

it simply assumed that I was busy. It was a stock email that goes to everyone who signs up for the trial. The marketers at this company believe that *everyone* is busy. We have gotten so preoccupied with being busy that even marketers assume we are not getting back to them because we have too much to do.

And I got a big kick out of this email: "I realize you're busy dealing with one thousand other things, but based upon your data and what's going on in the industry as a whole, I wanted to reach out immediately." One thousand things? How do they know? Are they exaggerating? Or do they really think people have one thousand things on their action list? Just for the record, if they do, that's too many.

Busy Is the New Default

Busy can have negative connotations. It may mean that we are busy with unimportant activities. Or maybe it means that we have too many projects on our plate. Maybe it just means that we overschedule ourselves. Or maybe we're too busy to tell people how busy we are.

For many, busy also has positive connotations. Busy is becoming the default state in Corporate America. We are expected to be busy. If we are not, it's assumed by bosses, colleagues, and customers that we are not producing, that we are not worthy of praise, that we are not worthy of promotions, that we are not worthy of financial success.

If this is the expectation and everyone is doing it, it forces others to request more of us. It's an infinite loop and a domino effect.

Let's face it, the volume of requests for our time exceeds our capacity to deal with all of them. If we were to put every request for our time on a to-do list, we would have more to do than we can possibly accomplish in a lifetime. Email, ding. Text, buzz. Phone, ring. Facebook notification, clang. Knock on the door, bang. There are more requests than we can possibly deal with, and the burden spills into other areas of our life. We find it difficult to step away for a few hours or a few days without responding.

The Problem with To-Do Lists

How do we process all of these requests? Most of us simply add requests to our to-do lists and try to multitask in an attempt to get everything done. A to-do list is a catalog of activities that you have committed to. To-do lists are usually a mix of urgent items that need to get done today and non-urgent items that can be done anytime; they also include less important tasks such as "email Bill" and big, multistep projects such as "reorganize department." Sometimes the items include target dates, and sometimes they do not.

There are several problems with to-do lists:

1 **They don't tell us what we need to do next.** If you have fifty items on your to-do list, which one will you do first? What is the decision-making process for making that choice: Will you tackle the first one on the list, the most important, the most urgent, the easiest, or the hardest?

2 **They include items that can't actually be completed.** For example, writing a book. Before I actually started writing a book, I thought about it for a long time. And the reason I was not making progress is that I didn't identify the next step. What I actually had to do to make progress on it was

to define the next step. For me, that next step was to sign up for a workshop. That workshop gave me a process, and then it flowed. When you see the complexity of the action that you need to complete, you have to take time to break it down and figure it out. What you need to do in that moment is make a decision about the action required to make progress on that activity.

3   **The items we put on them are not necessarily actionable.** For example, if "book" is on your list, the action associated with that could be "buy a book," "read a book," or maybe "write a book." The easier we can make it for ourselves to know the action, the easier it will be to execute it at the appropriate time. We don't have time in the heat of the battle, with so many things vying for our attention, to make that decision.

4   **They are usually not prioritized.** When we look at an unprioritized list, we need to make decisions in the moment on which task to focus on first. Sometimes we get lucky and choose the right one; at other times we choose the easiest one or the one that is the most actionable.

We cannot expect our brains to navigate all of this complexity. Tackling a to-do list requires us to make several decisions, and we would be better served if we made those decisions each time an item goes on our list. A to-do list that suffers from one or all of these problems makes it more likely that we will lose focus, and when we're unfocused, we're lulled into multitasking.

The greatest
enemy of
good thinking
is busyness.

JOHN C. MAXWELL

We Are All Multitasking

The question is, how effective is multitasking? Many believe that by multitasking we can get more done quickly. Today's technology makes it even easier for us to do that with a computer keyboard in one hand and a phone or tablet in the other.

To test the effectiveness of multitasking, Stanford University researchers compared two groups of people: those who engage in regular multitasking and those who do not.[1] They ran three experiments. First, they tested the ability to filter information by asking each group to remember the positions of blue rectangles on a screen after they had been removed and red rectangles added. The single-minded group had an easy time doing this, while the heavy multitaskers failed miserably.

The researchers also tested the heavy multitaskers to determine if they had better memories in a second experiment. They asked both groups to identify which letter sequences (for example, "AX") made a repeat appearance in a sequence of letters. Again, the single-minded group outperformed the high multitaskers.

Finally, in a third test, the researchers tested the heavy multitaskers' ability to switch from one task to another. This time they asked both groups to focus on a string of letters and numbers and to distinguish either the odd from the even numbers *or* the consonants from the vowels. In this case, the high multitaskers still underperformed.

I have news for you: multitasking is an illusion. What you are actually doing when you try to multitask is fast task switching.

Let me drive this point home by explaining how a computer works. The term "multitasking" first came from the world of computing. The central processing unit (CPU) is responsible for every request a user makes of the computer. From a keyboard stroke to complex calculations to intensive gaming, the

CPU manages it all. It is like the mind of the computer. When the CPU spends more time swapping between requests than it does processing requests, this is called thrashing. When a computer thrashes, either performance degrades significantly or the computer crashes. The same phenomenon happens to people when they are confronted with an excessive volume of requests: their ability to stay focused is jeopardized.

Let's try an exercise.[2] Set your stopwatch and then write the numbers 1 to 12 in a row as quickly as possible from left to right:

1 2 3 4 5 6 7 8 9 10 11 12

How long did that take you?

Set your stopwatch again and write the following as quickly as possible from left to right:

MULTITASKING

How long did that take you?

Now set your stopwatch one final time. This time, alternate between MULTITASKING and the numbers 1 to 12 left to right:

M 1 U 2 L 3 T, and so on

How long did that take you? My guess is it took you longer than the combination of the first two. Same work, same effort, but it took you longer when you switched between tasks.

The truth is that you can do more than one thing at the same time; you just can't give more than one thing at a time your attention. That's the difference.

Do you get it? Multitasking does not work. By doing less, we can accomplish more.

In September 2014, the University of Sussex in Brighton, England, conducted a study with seventy-five healthy

By doing less we might actually accomplish more and maintain our brain health.

adults.[3] The researchers looked at their personalities using a Media-Multitasking Index that they created for the study, and MRI scans. What they found was fascinating. Participants who reported higher amounts of media multitasking had smaller gray-matter density in the anterior cingulate cortex. This part of the brain is responsible for empathy, impulse control, emotional mastery, and decision making. This means that there are long-term impacts of multitasking on our ability to feel empathy, to control our impulses, and to master our emotions. This is true not just in the moment, but also in the long term. In other words, if you ever wonder about the reason you lose control of your emotions, check in on how much multitasking you are doing. Atrophy in this part of the brain also impacts your decision-making ability, which is critical to your ability to be productive.

By doing less, we might accomplish more *and* maintain our brain health.

Feeling Overwhelmed, Not Empowered

We think solutions such as to-do lists and multitasking are helping us be more productive, but they actually cause us to feel more overwhelmed rather than empowered.

Have you ever seen that Bob Newhart video where he plays a psychologist-therapist treating a patient who is afraid of being buried in a box? His advice to her is simply two words: "*Stop it!*" What he's getting at, by way of humor, is that sometimes we need to stop doing or thinking about something without looking for a complex solution. Feeling overwhelmed is not a condition or a state based in reality. It is simply the way we *feel*. That feeling comes from not making decisions about requests for our time. We defer a decision, and the next one, and the next one, and soon we have a whole pile of decisions that need to be made, and we're not sure which one to make next. That is being overwhelmed.

So, I have two words for you: *Stop it!*

Think about your list of projects like your dinner plate. We can fit only so many things on our dinner plate. Our eyes are often bigger than our stomach, and we put more on our plate than we can consume. When that happens, we feel stuffed, we can't move; all we want to do is sit on the couch. When we follow a diet, however, we have a process for deciding what goes on our dinner plate. The decision is made easy for us either through prepackaged items or lists outlining what we can and cannot eat. And if we follow the diet, we have more energy, we feel focused, and we're more productive.

The same thing can happen with our project plate. When we are conscious about what goes on our project plate, we can focus, we feel light, we feel productive, and things get done. When we have too many things on our project plate, we feel overwhelmed, are not productive, and can be frozen by inaction.

The similarities between eating too much and being overwhelmed are compelling. And I believe the solutions are the same. We need to know what to put on our project plate and in the right quantities. Most importantly, we need to know when to do this. Remember, this is a when-to book, not a how-to book.

When we can go beyond feeling overwhelmed, we can start being productive. We can't just stop feeling something, however. We need to replace it with another feeling. So what would be a better way to feel? Productive, energized, empowered, determined, grounded, confident, capable, decisive? When we transform that feeling from being overwhelmed to one of these words, we will start to make decisions.

Think about it: Do you make more decisions when you are feeling overwhelmed, burned out, or worried? Or do you make more decisions when you are feeling empowered? How is it serving you to sit on the couch *thinking* about how much you have to do? Do something. Make a decision. Check something off the list. You will create momentum that will quickly dissolve that feeling of being overwhelmed.

Think of a time you felt upset about something someone did or said. Maybe it was about politics or religion or something you are passionate about. Your blood was boiling and you may have lost your cool. That situation caused you to be upset, right? The truth is, no one else controls your emotions. We decide how to respond to a situation. "Between stimulus and response, there is a space. In that space lies our freedom and our power to choose our response. In our response lies our growth and our happiness."[4] We get to choose whether we want to feel overwhelmed or empowered.

KEY PRODUCTIVITY POINTS

- Multitasking is an illusion. You are really fast task switching.

- To-do lists often do not work because they are not prioritized and not actionable.

- If you are feeling overwhelmed, there is a reliable way to overcome that and feel more empowered.

Some people think they are thinking when they are merely rearranging their prejudices.

BISHOP WILLIAM FITZJAMES OLDHAM

Be Purposely Productive

MANY EXPERTS TELL us that in order to be productive rather than busy, we need to say no. The idea of saying no is nothing new. Many productivity experts talk about the importance of saying no, and many others teach you how to say no. But no one wants to say no. We know that we need to say no; we know how to say no. All of that is important, but the key factor is when to say yes. And that is what I want to help you with. Before we dive into the details of when to say yes, however, we to need to explore how to change our mindset so we can transform being endlessly busy into being what I call "purposely productive."

Change the Language of Work and Life

In Chapter One, I talked about how everyone is busy, and that busyness is taking over our lives. The opposite of being busy is being purposely productive. When you are purposely productive, you have a feeling of confidence that you are in control, getting things done, and staying on task. It means that you are making progress on your most important goals.

Purposely productive means you are crystal clear on your goals, you know your most important goal, you know when you will accomplish it, and you know exactly what the end result will look like.

Purposely productive is that feeling you have at the end of the day when you have accomplished so much that you feel good about relaxing and spending time with your loved ones without giving your work a second thought.

Purposely productive also means that you are achieving your goals. To achieve your goals, you must make a decision to focus on your goals and to focus on activities that support your goals. We can all be busy. We can all keep ourselves busy responding to other people's requests. We can all keep our calendars full. The difference when we are purposely productive is that we decide to focus on achieving our goals. You may actually decide not to check anything off your action list today. Maybe you want to do nothing. Maybe you want to enjoy time with the family. Well, this is still useful and valuable.

Purposely productive means that you are conscious about how you invest your time. You decide how to use your time; other people don't do it for you. You're not accepting phone calls, text messages, notifications, or emails as a default. You are fully present when you do what you do.

To summarize, you are purposely productive when you are

- crystal clear on your goals;
- feeling in control;
- making progress on your most important goals;
- achieving your goals; and
- conscious about how to invest your time.

A *HuffPost* article titled "10 Words to Use Instead of 'Busy'" suggests these alternatives: intentionally full, abundant, rich, engaged, wholehearted, captivated, productive, resplendent, dynamic, and excited.[1] Such great words that have a much better connotation than "busy." Which of those words resonates with you most? When someone asks you, "How are you?" what response will you share now?

Here's the difference between busy and purposely productive:

BUSY	PURPOSELY PRODUCTIVE
Too much to do	Curated, purposeful priorities
Feeling out of control	Feeling in control
Falling behind	Making progress
Reactive	Proactive
A full schedule	A few priorities
Thinking and saying "I'm busy"	Thinking and saying "I'm purposely productive"
Multitasking	Single-focused
Checking email	Processing email
Feeling overwhelmed	Feeling empowered

I hope you're starting to see how we can transform our lives from being busy to being purposely productive. The change in language alone can make a difference, and when we start living this way, the opportunity will arise to make better decisions about what we focus on. Once you've changed the way you think and talk about your work and your life, you're set to make better decisions. Next, I will lay the groundwork for how to evaluate requests for your time, by showing you how to make better decisions.

Reflective Decisions Are Better Decisions

The most productive people make better decisions. They are thoughtful about their decisions. For purposely productive people, decisions are not taken lightly, and they are not made in a passive or reactive way.

Research shows a connection between reflection and effective decision making. Try this test: "A ball and a bat cost $1.10. The bat costs $1.00 more than the ball. How much does the ball cost?"[2]

It's better to make the wrong decision than no decision at all.

DONALD E. KHOURI (MY FATHER)

The intuitive answer is ten cents, and when I first saw this word problem, that was my answer too. After some careful thought, you will recognize that the correct answer is five cents. Let me explain. The ball costs five cents. The bat costs $1.00 more than the ball. So, the bat costs $1.05.

$0.05 + $1.05 = $1.10

In an experiment, those who answered this question and two others correctly were more likely to make better decisions about investing or spending their money, because they were more thoughtful.[3]

Our time works the same way. When we stop to think, we make better decisions about where to invest our time. People who are more reflective and more patient make better decisions.

Have you ever seen viral math problems such as this on Facebook?

The first row is three clocks, two reading nine o'clock and one reading three o'clock. The sum is twenty-one. The second row is three calculators each displaying "1234." The sum is thirty. The third row is three light bulbs totaling fifteen. And the fourth row is the clock, the calculator, and the three light bulbs. The viewer's job is to figure out the answer.

Usually, there's an obvious answer that many people jump to. When you look more closely, you see the clocks have different faces, nine and three, that we must account for. And the calculator numbers change from 1234 to 1224, which changes the sum it represents. The light bulbs have five lines above them in the third equation and four lines in the last equation. Finally, we need to apply the correct order of operations (PEM-DAS). PEMDAS stands for parentheses first, then exponents, multiplication, division, addition, and subtraction. So, the multiplication will take place first in the fourth equation. We need to give it some additional thought before arriving at a decision, otherwise, our Facebook friend will post "incorrect" or "nope" or "try again."

Did you figure out the correct answer to this one? If you need to see the answer before continuing, here it is:

- First equation is 9 + 9 + 3 = 21 based on the clock readings.

- Second equation is 10 + 10 + 10 = 30 based on the calculator reading "1234."

- Third equation is 15 + 15 - 15 = 15 based on five lines above the lightbulb.

- Fourth equation is 9 + (9 x 36) since there are only four lines above the lightbulbs, and we can assume addition.

- So, 9 + 324 = 333. That's the answer.

What Gets in the Way of Making Better Decisions?

As human beings, we have several cognitive biases and limitations that get in the way of making better decisions. A cognitive bias is a way of thinking that steers us in one direction over others. In other words, we create an answer based on our subjective viewpoint versus objective, logical thought. When we let cognitive biases get in the way, we are not using good judgment and, therefore, not making ideal decisions. Let's look at a few cognitive biases that affect our decisions.

Sunk Cost Fallacy

A sunk cost is an investment you have made that you will not get back regardless of future decisions. For example, let's say you bought a $25 ticket to a buffet lunch. You go through once selecting some of your favorite foods. When you finish your plate, you are feeling pretty full. The question is, do you stop, feeling full and satisfied, or do you go back for a second round to get your money's worth? The $25 is spent either way. Which path will make you feel better: Getting a second plate and then maybe dessert, feeling overstuffed, and gaining weight? Or feeling good and satisfied that you got your money's worth?

A sunk cost is one that has already been incurred and will not be recovered. If a cost is already sunk, it should have no impact on our future decisions. Several years ago, I purchased tickets to a Billy Joel concert out in Worcester, Massachusetts, about forty-five miles from home. I bought two tickets for $150 for my friend and me, which was pretty significant for a college student at the time. As the day approached it was clear a snowstorm was arriving that evening. We had a decision to make: Do we drive in the snowstorm and realize the value of our investment or stay safe at home? Billy was not rescheduling the concert. First of all, we wanted to see him, and more importantly, we had invested $150. We didn't want to lose the investment. We went to the concert, and I'll never forget the drive home in the blizzard—significant snowfall with little plowing on the Massachusetts Turnpike. Fortunately, we made it safely, and I am here to write about it. The right thing to do would have been to stay home and be safe.

Finally, consider the airplane problem, which has two scenarios.[4]

Scenario A (Prior Investment): As the president of an airline company, you have invested $10 million of the company's money into a research project. The goal is to build a plane that will not be detected by conventional radar. When the project is 90 percent completed, another firm begins marketing a plane that cannot be detected by radar. Also, it is apparent that their plane is much faster and far more economical than the plane your company is building. The question is: Should you invest the last 10 percent of the research funds to finish your radar-blank plane?

Scenario B (No Prior Investment): As president of an airline company, you have received a suggestion from one of your employees. The suggestion is to use the last $1 million of your research funds to develop a plane that will not be detected by conventional radar. However, another firm has just begun marketing a plane that cannot be detected by radar. Also, it is apparent that their plane is much faster and far more economical than the plane your company could build. The question is: Should you invest the last million dollars of your research funds to build the radar-blank plane proposed by your employee?

Of course, the investment is exactly the same in both scenarios: $1 million. However, the way that most people respond to the questions is remarkably different. Eighty-five percent of people choose to invest the funds in Scenario A, while only 17 percent choose to do so in Scenario B. Although the investment is exactly the same in both scenarios, a large majority choose to invest in Scenario A as a result of the sunk cost bias. We somehow believe that the original investment should weigh on our future decisions. If we are making good decisions, however, we will not take that previous investment into account.

This applies to our time as well. The amount of time we have already invested in a project is considered a sunk cost and should have no bearing on whether we invest more time in that project. Later on, in Chapter Six, we will have the opportunity to evaluate the projects on our plate to see which ones should stay and which should be deprioritized or canceled.

Confirmation Bias

Confirmation bias is the tendency to seek out or interpret information that supports our predetermined beliefs and ideas. Take, for example, a jury in a high-profile case. Defense attorneys often seek an alternate venue to try the case and for jury selection on the grounds that if jurors have been exposed to media coverage of the crime, they will start to form an opinion of the defendant's guilt. During testimony, these jurors look for information and data that supports the defendant's guilt and ignore conflicting information.

How does this apply to decisions about investing your time? For example, say you attend a weekly recurring project-status meeting. If you believe that this meeting is beneficial to your career and moves you closer to your goals, you'll look for data to support that assumption. Or maybe you believe that saying no to the project your boss asked you to lead would be career limiting. You'll look for information to support that belief. That's confirmation bias.

Dunning-Kruger Effect

When I spoke to my teams at Fidelity Investments, sometimes two hundred strong, I was good at it. I'd share the organization's mission and goals and get team members excited about them. I'd field tough questions while being inspiring. When I left the corporate world and started speaking in front of groups of clients or potential clients, I thought I had it mastered.

Now, when I look at speaking videos from ten years ago, I know that I was not a great speaker. What I've learned since then from the great people at Heroic Public Speaking is that we need to treat our presentations like a performance: have a script, rehearse your script, know how to use your body, know how to answer questions the right way, and know how to make an audience *feel* something. I didn't know how unskilled I was because I didn't know what I didn't know.

Named after its creators, the Dunning-Kruger effect is a cognitive bias in which we believe we are better at something than we actually are. In one company, 32 percent of software engineers rated their own skills in the top 5 percent of their company, and in a second company, 42 percent did so.[5]

Overconfidence in our own abilities can impact our productivity by causing us to take on projects we believe we can excel at and make commitments we cannot keep since we don't have the skills. Sometimes, we are reluctant to ask for help on these projects and fall behind.

When we let cognitive biases get in the way, we are not using good judgment and, therefore, not making ideal decisions.

Gambler's Fallacy

Early in my technology career, I programmed on computer hardware called Stratus. Stratus computers were fault tolerant, which means they couldn't crash. They were designed and built with two of everything—two disk drives, two CPUs, two memory boards. If one of them failed, the other took over its function without any impact. Stratus computers were not supposed to crash. In one particular situation, however, ours did, fault tolerance and all. The experts came in, reviewed the situation, and explained what had happened. It was an error with the operating system, and if you understand computers at all, you'll know that the operating system cannot be duplicated. We had an important decision to make: Should we take the system down again to apply the fix, or should we wait until the weekend, when we'd have more flexibility for an outage? The guidance we received was that there was a one-in-a-million chance of the bug occurring again. So, we decided to take those odds and wait until the weekend. Can you guess what happened? *The Stratus crashed again.* In reality, the probability was much higher than the experts communicated because of the way our applications were pushing the operating system.

In the gambler's fallacy, we believe that a certain outcome will or won't happen, without determining the probability.[6] Here's a simple example: If we flip a coin nine times and get heads nine times straight, we may believe that a tail is much more likely to appear on the tenth flip. In reality, the tenth flip has exactly the same odds of being heads as any other flip, which is 50 percent.

This cognitive bias is in action when we evaluate requests for our time because we think, *This time, this task will be easier,* or *This time, I won't have to stay late,* or *This time, I won't hit the roadblocks I usually do.*

Planning Fallacy

Have you ever planned out your day to get one hundred (or fifty or twenty) things accomplished, and you got only half done? You are not alone. Another one of our mental blocks as humans is tending to underestimate how much time something will take. You bring six books on vacation, you anticipate cutting employee turnover in half, your general contractor says he can get the renovation done in three months, your wife says she can have a baby in seven. Okay, maybe not the last one, but you get the idea. Overlooking the planning fallacy will often result in time overruns, cost overruns, and fewer benefits than anticipated.

This is one of the biggest reasons we take on too much. We think we can do it all.

I have some bad news and some good news regarding this bias. The bad news is that awareness of the bias does not help all that much. Even when we know about the planning fallacy, we still underestimate time. The good news is that it applies only when we are estimating our own work. It does not apply to others. We can use this to our benefit by asking someone knowledgeable to help us estimate our projects or tasks. This will help us get closer to having a manageable project list.

Outcome Bias

Sometimes we evaluate the quality of a past decision based on the outcome. For example, you may think, *I'm so glad I decided to invest in that stock, because it doubled in value.* Well, maybe that's the right decision, and maybe you got lucky.

Let me share another example from the world of poker. Let's say I'm playing Texas Hold'em. In Texas Hold'em players are dealt two cards, and I'm dealt two queens. This is a premium hand. I raise before the first three common cards (the flop) are revealed, and two other players call (match) my bet. The flop is ace, king, two. One of the callers leads betting, the other folds. It's uncommon for someone other than the raiser to make the first bet during a round of betting. So, this bet should be a flag that something is up. The lead bettor on the flop may have an ace or a king. With no other information about the style of the player, it's a good assumption. Well, I decide to call anyway and get a queen on the turn (the fourth common card). Now, I have three queens (also known as a set) and likely the best hand. The river (the fifth and last common card) is an irrelevant card, and sure enough I win the hand and the pot.

I made the right decision, right? After all, I won the pot. Nooo, this was not the right decision. The odds of hitting one of the two remaining queens was 4 percent; 4.3 percent, to be exact. That means the pot would have to yield twenty-three times the bet, and that is usually not likely. The result does *not* validate the decision, the process does.

Decision Fatigue

We make better decisions earlier in the day than we do later in the day.

"Hi honey, welcome home. What should we order for dinner?"

"You decide. I'll eat anything."

"No really, I'm flexible, whatever you want."

"I can't make one more decision today."

That's decision fatigue. If your spouse had asked you first thing in the morning what you wanted to order for dinner that night, it would have been an easy decision. But you've been making decisions all day long that affect people's lives, their businesses, or their wallets. This simple yet important dinner decision is now over the top.

So, we need to find ways to make the important decisions early in the day and defer important decisions until a time when we are not experiencing decision fatigue.

Another way decision fatigue manifests itself is in how we deal with ambiguity, which is prevalent in many requests for our time. If you don't have all the information to make a good decision, you'll experience more and more ambiguity as you take on more responsibility. Consider this situation. You need to decide whether to attend a conference. Your schedule is not nailed down for those days. The conference is during a demanding time of the year, and you may need to be local to adapt to what is needed. The timing of the conference also aligns with the launch of a new product, if all stays on schedule. If you were to choose one conference all year long, this would be the one. The deadline to register is Friday. This is ambiguity: you do not have all the information to make a perfect decision, yet making a decision now is necessary given the deadline. We are better off making these decisions earlier in the day when we can process all of the ambiguity more easily.

Cognitive Miser Theory

Finally, in order to make good decisions, we need to recognize that because we are limited in our capacity to process information, we often take shortcuts. This is known as the cognitive miser theory.[7] You know by now that "cognitive" relates to the act of processing information. A miser is someone who spends as little as possible or, in this case, uses little effort. Taken together, it means we want to think less.

Sometimes saying yes to a request for our time is a shortcut or the easier way out. If we say no, we may need to justify it; we may need to explain the reasons behind our answer. This approach can lead to undesired results. Think about it: if we say yes to everything because it is the easy way out, because it is a shortcut, because it is the path of least resistance, we are going to have too many things on our plate and not serve any of our requesters in the way we desire. Now, I know that no one actually reading this book has too many things on their plate. Yeah, right.

PRODUCTIVITY CORNER
Recognize Cognitive Biases

For one week, when you consider requests for your time, be aware of the cognitive biases. Are you looking for data to support your idea (confirmation bias)? For example, a colleague asks you to attend a meeting. Challenge your assumptions that you should automatically accept the request. What may be a reason not to accept the request?

Are you overestimating your competency in a certain area, or would you need some help (Dunning-Kruger effect)? Are you underestimating how long something may take you to complete (planning fallacy)?

Give your decisions slightly more time than you normally would. Instead of jumping to an answer, reflect on the decision for a couple of minutes or more.

The Importance of Thoughtful Decisions

Biases are a reality, and we cannot eliminate them. However, we can increase the likelihood of making better decisions by becoming critical thinkers—by being aware of these biases and limitations and challenging them.

Being busy rather than productive stems from an inability to make decisions. An email appears in your inbox, you open it, and it says there is a cool webinar happening next week. It is on the exact topic you've been thinking about, and it will change your life. So, you immediately close the email and think, *I'll sign up for that later.* Or a client asks you to help respond to an unusual situation with an employee. That email will stay in your inbox along with the 5,432 other ones you haven't made a decision on yet. Maybe you'll make a decision when it becomes a fire.

Although it might feel easier to postpone the decision until later, in the long run it's much easier to make the decision in the moment rather than putting it off, and I've developed the Five Steps to Protect Your Time to make it even easier.

Other authors may encourage you *not* to think about your decisions before acting. "Just do it," they say. That may work for some people. In my research, however, what I learned about the most productive people is that they make excellent, thoughtful decisions. This may not seem intuitive because we see productive people making many seemingly quick decisions. In reality, the most productive people depend as much on their unconscious mind as their conscious mind.

Conscious thought is what you are consciously aware of when you execute a task or project or make a decision. Unconscious thought, on the other hand, comprises the relevant processes that take place outside conscious awareness, and it has significantly more capacity than conscious thought.[8] We can hold only five to seven things in our conscious mind at any one time. Although the original source is unclear, Sigmund Freud has been credited with comparing the mind to an iceberg: "The mind is like an iceberg; it floats with one-seventh of

Being busy rather than productive stems from an inability to make decisions.

its bulk above the water." The conscious mind is the tip of the iceberg above the water. The unconscious mind is the much larger piece below the water. In other words, our subconscious mind is capable of so much more than our conscious mind, when we put it to good use. It's virtually unlimited.

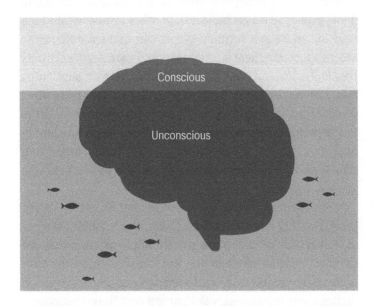

We can direct our subconscious mind to handle complex decision making. You've heard the expression, "Sleep on it." That is putting your subconscious mind to work on those complex topics. Ask yourself a question before you go to bed, and you'll likely wake up with an important revelation about that question. In his book *Thinking, Fast and Slow,* Daniel Kahneman describes two different ways the brain forms thoughts. System one (subconscious) is fast, automatic, frequent, emotional, and stereotypic. System one is in operation when we solve two plus two, drive a car, or read text on a billboard. System two (conscious) is slow, effortful, infrequent, logical, and calculating. It is in operation when we focus on a conversation with someone at a party, walk faster than usual, give someone our phone number, or park in a tight space. It is purposeful.

Making a decision is making a choice. Sometimes it is a choice between doing something or not doing something, or doing project A versus project B. In other words, within each decision there is a conflict. When you make a decision to accept a request, there is an opportunity cost. An opportunity cost is the lost opportunity to make progress on something else. You may need to take something else off your plate when you accept a new request (we will explore this in more detail in Chapter Six), or you may just spend less time on another important project. So, the conflict is, where do you invest your time now: in the existing project or the new project? How do you stay focused?

Think about a time when you were laser focused on something. How did that feel? Did you lose track of time? What types of results did you get? Many people would say that they are the most productive when they are focused. One of the most successful projects I led as a software program manager was converting users from a legacy system to a new, improved system. It was my singular focus. I was leading a cross-organizational, cross-functional group of software teams that had to make changes to their systems to make it all work. Because it was my singular focus, I could anticipate delays, remove bottlenecks, and support the other leaders (who were not as focused on one project) in getting the work done. This project had visibility to the most senior levels of the organization. I could look at data differently, slice and dice it, to understand what was going on. I also reported regularly to senior managers and could provide clear, concise updates because of the focus. That focus was created because I knew exactly when to say yes. Would the request move us closer to finishing this project? If so, I could make myself available. If not, I pointed the requester in the right direction. Who was making the request? How clear was the request? How did it fit in with our other priorities? Having clarity on when to say yes made the decision-making process much easier.

When you gain that clarity, you will be more able to focus on the important projects and deprioritize the others. In the next section, I will show you when to say yes using the Five Steps to Protect Your Time. For each step, you will build the framework needed to make important, reflective decisions in the moment. I will ask you to do some upfront planning so that you have everything you need in the future to say yes at the right time. Let's dive into it.

KEY PRODUCTIVITY POINTS

- Reflective decisions are better decisions.

- There are several cognitive biases that get in our way of making purposely productive decisions:

  - Sunk cost fallacy
  - Confirmation bias
  - Dunning-Kruger effect
  - Planning fallacy
  - Outcome bias
  - Decision fatigue
  - Cognitive miser theory

- To ensure your decision making is productive

  - be thoughtful and utilize the power of your unconscious mind—use system one;
  - be aware of your cognitive biases;
  - understand the opportunity cost; and
  - consider the choice you are making.

- Focus on the important things, which is exactly what I'll help you with in the next section.

PART TWO

The Five Steps to Protect Your Time

The successful leader must plan his work and work his plan.

NAPOLEON HILL

Create Your Roadmap

1
Create your
roadmap

2
Define your
relationship hierarchy

3
Assess the quality
of the request

4
Prioritize and
reprioritize

5
Master
delegation

OUR HOME RENOVATION project started with a desire to have two sinks in the master bath. Then we decided to make some changes to the living room; specifically, we wanted to convert the wood-burning fireplace to a gas fireplace. Next, I decided my home office needed updating, and we designed a built-in bookcase (which I love, by the way). Ultimately, we decided to touch every room in the house. We renovated all three bathrooms, repainted the whole house, renovated the kitchen with a completely new layout, and added the built-in bookcase and a storage cabinet to my home office. It was quite extensive. Before the contractor did any work, the first thing we did was build a roadmap. Before any nail was hammered or any drill was spun, we created a plan. We hired a designer who helped us figure out what we wanted—from the redesign of the kitchen, to where the recessed lights would go, to the placement of the furniture. Then, we divided the project into three phases. We had a picture of what the end would look like, and we had a roadmap to get there.

The Power of Planning

If you were going on a trip, say driving from Boston to New York, you would use a roadmap. That could be the old-fashioned kind that you unfold or an app on your device. The map would show you exactly where you are going, which route to take, and roughly how long it will take to get there. You may hit some obstacles along the way: traffic, weather, and maybe even highway patrol. When you hit traffic, what do you do? Do you give up, turn around, and go back to where you started? Do you get off at the nearest exit and go sightseeing? No, you either sit and wait it out or you search for a better route. You may also talk on the phone, or listen to music or an audiobook, which helps you enjoy the journey. You stay focused on your destination; you stay the course. The roadmap keeps you on track.

Staying the course seems simple when expressed in these terms. When it comes to our goals, one of four things can happen:

- We may not have a roadmap.

- We have a roadmap, but we get discouraged by obstacles.

- We get attracted to the next greatest thing and follow a route that leads away from the destination.

- We don't intentionally enjoy the journey.

So how do we avoid going off course? To use another travel metaphor, when a plane is traveling to a destination, it is off course over 90 percent of the time. But the pilot knows where he's going and will adjust continually to get back on course.

So, the first step in knowing when to say yes is knowing where you're going—designing your roadmap.

Give this some thought. *Where* do you want to be in three years? *Who* do you want to be in three years? Let's imagine you were just awarded the top award in your industry for outstanding achievement. What is "outstanding achievement" for you? What did you accomplish, and who have you become? Let's take this a step further. What if you were celebrating your hundredth birthday and looking back at your successful life. What does that life look like? Again, what did you accomplish, where did you go, what difference did you make in your world, and what did you acquire? Can you create a visual of that end point?

To see the Five Steps in action and how they all hinge on having a roadmap, let's look at *It's a Wonderful Life,* my favorite movie. It was nominated for five Academy Awards, including Best Picture, Best Actor, and Best Director. I watch it every year, usually around Christmas time, and I love watching it with friends who are seeing it for the first time. There is something special about it that is inspirational and helps you appreciate your life's journey.

The movie opens on Christmas Eve, with many people praying for the protagonist, George Bailey (played by Jimmy Stewart), because he seems to be in some kind of trouble. Later we learn that he attempted to kill himself because his uncle Billy, his business partner, lost $8,000 in cash. The heavenly bodies deliberate on how to respond to all of these prayers. They decide to ask Clarence, an angel who has not yet earned his wings, to intervene for George. The first half of the movie is a flashback, with the heavenly bodies replaying George's life so Clarence will know whom he's helping.

George faces many difficult decisions in his life. First, we see him at the age of twelve deciding whether to tell his boss, a pharmacist, that he'd put potentially lethal ingredients in the pills for a young patient. He ultimately does tell him before the pills are distributed, saving the boy's life, and it builds a bond between George and the pharmacist that lasts a lifetime.

We see George's love for travel early on when he references *National Geographic* and Fiji, Tahiti, and the Coral Sea. He refers to himself as an explorer and declares that he will explore the world someday. In that same scene, his friend Mary

A good plan
today is better
than a perfect
plan tomorrow.

secretly whispers, "George Bailey, I'll love you till the day I die." That's clearly her roadmap.

A few scenes later, George is walking with Mary and again shares his dreams or roadmap with her. They are throwing rocks at an abandoned house, and the idea is that if they can break a window, their wish will come true. When George breaks a window, Mary asks him what he wished for. George says,

> Not just one wish, a whole hat full. Mary, I know what I am going to do tomorrow, and the next day, and next year and the year after that. I'm shakin' the dust of this crummy little town off my feet and I'm gonna see the world. Italy, Greece, the Parthenon, the Colosseum. Then I'm comin' back here to go to college to see what they know. And then I'm gonna build things. I'm gonna build airfields, I'm gonna build skyscrapers a hundred stories high, I'm gonna build bridges a mile long.

George is clear about his roadmap. He knows what he wants to accomplish and how and when he wants to accomplish it. Still a young man, George is already thinking like a highly productive executive.

The Mindset of the Most Productive People

When I spoke with senior technology professionals such as CIOs and CTOs, they shared their mindset when they evaluated a request for their time, including matching the request to what was already on their roadmap. One showed me a roadmap that he used to make sure he allocated his time appropriately. The roadmap was a one-page, color-coded document. It showed projects in boxes aligned with time on the horizontal axis, and organizational priorities aligned with effort on the vertical axis.

He explained, "This is the roadmap. We have long-term, three-plus years, and [this year] is more detailed. The size of the box is relative to the effort and timing." The map depicted the next three years, and the current year had the most detail. The size of the boxes correlated with the effort and timing.

One of my executive coaching clients—I'll call him Adam—has a goal to be the chief financial officer in his company or another company. He has an interim milestone to be the full controller in eighteen months, and he has identified specific skills he will need to master to attain that promotion. He knows specifically how big his team will be and the reasons that path is important to him. So, the next six quarters are mapped out on his roadmap.

Robert, the CTO of an Ivy League school, said that his true filter for requests was his set of goals. If a request aligned with the goals, he would accept; otherwise, it would require more justification. "Create goals; long-term, medium-term, and short-term goals. And use that as the filter to determine how you prioritize things and what you throw off. So, in terms of my true filter mechanism... it really comes back to goals."

James, the CIO of a financial services firm, made sure the requests are related to his "mission at work."

To illustrate how having a roadmap is the key to protecting your time, let's imagine we're getting into our car to drive from the East Coast to California. To make the trip effective, we would first need to know where we are going—Los Angeles or San Francisco or San Diego? We need to have our destination in mind. We will also need to know how long we want the drive to take. We may decide we want to arrive as quickly as possible, and we will rotate drivers so that we can be on the road most of the day and night. Or, we may want to make several stops along the way and enjoy the cities. Or maybe something in between, like drive during the day and sleep at night. The approach we take will influence our decisions. Perhaps we need to plan hotel stops or sightseeing adventures. The roadmap could look something like this:

Day 1–2: Boston to Niagara Falls. Spend one day in Niagara.
Day 3–4: Niagara to Chicago. Spend two days in Chicago.
Day 5–6: Chicago to Iowa. Visit friends.
Day 7: Iowa to Kansas City.
Day 8: Kansas City to Denver.
Day 9–10: Denver to Las Vegas. Spend one day in Las Vegas.
Day 11: Las Vegas to Los Angeles. Arrive.

DAY 1–2	DAY 3–4	DAY 5–6	DAY 7	DAY 8	DAY 9–10	DAY 11
Boston Niagara	Chicago	Iowa	Kansas City	Denver	Las Vegas	Los Angeles

It could look like the above map. Now, imagine if a friend from Florida texted you and said, "Heard you're taking a cross-country trip! We'd love to have you for a few days, swing by on your way." That will significantly change your roadmap. Will you stay the course or reroute and replan? Perhaps you love Iowa and want to stay longer. Will you adjust your plans?

When I spoke with senior leaders, two of them provided examples of a request where they imagined they had no choice and, ultimately, chose to leave the organization. Now, this does not mean you have to say yes to keep your job. Quite the contrary. I advocate strongly in this book that we all need to be more selective about our yeses. We must provide practical, compelling reasons for saying no to a request. In these examples, the requests were more than simply roadmap alignment questions. The requests conflicted with personal values, and after much deliberation, the participants realized that their choice was to comply with the request and compromise their values or leave the organization. That's how committed they were to their roadmap.

How does the roadmap work in practice? Say I receive a request from a friend to go out for a hot fudge sundae. I could say yes because I want to be with my friend, or I could say no because eating a hot fudge sundae does not align with the roadmap. But there's another choice. I could say, "Let's do something else," so that I can be with my friend and stick to my goal.

PRODUCTIVITY CORNER
Build Your Roadmap

What could your roadmap look like? Which categories would you create? What are your big initiatives in the next twelve months?

To get you started, think about your roadmap in three dimensions—time, size, and category. For example, let's break down your next three years into phases leading you to that outstanding achievement award. What would have to happen in year one, year two, and year three for you to end up at that awards ceremony? Go ahead and sketch it out.

Now let's break down year one. As we develop our own roadmap, we want to think in months and quarters versus days. What would have to happen in each quarter—Q1, Q2, Q3, and Q4—for you to accomplish your year one goal? Next, break down the first quarter, the first three months. What would have to happen in month one, month two, and month three to get where you need to be at the end of Q1?

Now, if you lay everything out in a roadmap, it might look something like the diagram on the following page.

I have quarters of the year across the top, life categories along the side, and the goals of each entered in the roadmap.

	Q1	Q2	Q3	Q4
	GOAL 1	GOAL 2	GOAL 3	GOAL 4
BUSINESS	Hire 10 people by March 31			
	Website development	Website launch	Implement email marketing	Expand social media presence
	Acquire 6 new clients	Acquire 6 new clients	Acquire 6 new clients	Acquire 6 new clients
	Learn new skillset			
PHYSICAL	Lose 10 pounds by March 30	Reduce body fat	Update wardrobe	
TIME	Learn the Five Steps to protect my time	Implement the Five Steps	Master the Five Steps	Be purposely productive
	Block time in schedule for goals			

For now, capture your high-level goals, and in the next section of this chapter you will have the opportunity to create more detailed goals. The first category may be "Business." In this example, the goal is to hire ten people by March 31. This is identified in the first quarter. You may also have a category called "Time." Since you're reading this book, you could chunk learning the Five Steps into smaller pieces. For example, in the first quarter, you could have "Learn the Five Steps to Protect Your Time"; in the second quarter, "Implement them"; in the third quarter, "Master them"; and by the fourth quarter you are purposely productive.

To help you build your own roadmap, I've designed a template that can be downloaded from WhenToSayYes.com. Keep in mind that your roadmap does not need to be perfect the first time through. Think of it as a living document that you can update over time. A good plan today is better than a perfect plan tomorrow. Print it out and keep it front and center, or have the digital version in a place where you can review it periodically. Know it well.

Khouri's Seven Cs of Goal Setting

Now that you have a preliminary roadmap, you'll need to be more specific about your goals. Many of you have heard of SMART goals. SMART is an acronym that has many different meanings:

Specific
Measurable
Achievable, Attainable, or Agreed Upon
Realistic, Relevant, or Reasonable
Time-bound, Timely, or Time-based

This is a great goal-setting model, and I have used it for many years. I realized, however, in thinking about how to draft a roadmap, that there are gaps in the model.

First, I never understood the difference between specific and measurable. Can a goal be measurable but not specific? What else makes it specific? Who wants a goal to be realistic anyway? Was Steve Jobs realistic? Oprah? Warren Buffett? I doubt it. They broke all the rules. Goals must be timely, but you'll see when I share my improved system that being timely is not enough.

When you can set a goal that meets all the criteria of Khouri's Seven Cs, you'll know you have a solid goal.

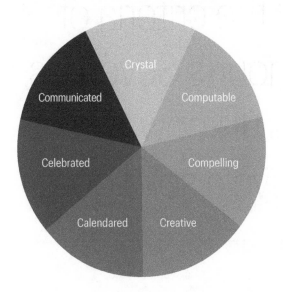

Crystal

Make sure the goal is crystal clear—it is understandable to yourself and others. Anyone working on the goal, reviewing the goal, or interested in the goal must be able to comprehend

When you can set a goal that meets all the criteria of Khouri's Seven Cs, you'll know you have a solid goal.

it easily. When something is crystal clear, it is transparent, unambiguous, and completely understood. Avoid acronyms and industry lingo, which can be confusing and less specific.

Do you remember the scene from *A Few Good Men* when Colonel Jessep, played by Jack Nicholson, is on the stand responding to questions from Lieutenant Daniel Kaffee, played by Tom Cruise? He says, "We follow orders, son, we follow orders or people die. It's that simple. Are we clear?"

Kaffee responds, "Yes sir."

"Are we clear?" Jessep asks again, more firmly and loudly.

"Crystal," Kaffee says.

Which reminds me of a weekend with great friends on Cape Cod. We planned dinner Saturday night at the Dan'l Webster Inn, a prestigious restaurant and hotel on the Cape. We spent the day sightseeing and shopping. We were famished by the time dinner rolled around. We all ordered some of our favorite dishes, and my friend's nine-year-old daughter, Michelle, ordered mac and cheese, which was the only thing familiar and tempting to her on the menu. In her nine-year-old mind, the only mac and cheese she knew was Kraft Mac and Cheese (you know, the boxed, orange mac and cheese). It is plain, simple, and comforting. So, when the server brought the *white* mac and cheese topped with breadcrumbs and green onions, you could see the surprise on her face.

Many nine-year-olds would have cried, yelled, or thrown the food back at the server. Not Michelle. "I should have been more specific," she exclaimed, and we all erupted in laughter that this nine-year-old had the presence of mind to realize her lack of specificity had delivered an undesired result.

When setting goals, being specific is being crystal clear.

Example: *I want to lose weight* is so clear, unambiguous, and understandable that a third grader would grasp it.

Computable

How will you know when the goal is complete? If a goal is not computable or quantifiable, we have no way of knowing that we have accomplished it or if we are making progress. Make each goal quantifiable in some way. Put a number on it so you can compute the results.

Example: I want to lose *ten pounds*. We can measure ten pounds; we can't measure "weight."

Compelling

One of the key distinctions between those who achieve their goals and those who do not is that the former have a compelling reason to stay on track. If you don't have a compelling reason, the distractions will inhibit you from significant progress toward your goal. When you get bumped off your track, you won't have a compelling reason to get back on. When discovering your compelling reason, dig three levels deep. First ask, what is compelling about this goal? Next, ask, what is compelling about that? One more time, what is compelling about that? When you ask three times, something extremely compelling will emerge. Try it out.

Example: I want to lose ten pounds *so that I can look good in a bathing suit*. Perhaps the first pass of this was, "So that I can look good." Dig deeper: "So that I can look good in my clothes." Dig deeper, "So that I can look good in a bathing suit." Do you see how it gets more compelling each time?

When I lost thirty-five pounds in 2013, I had a compelling reason. My compelling reason was to stay off medication. I am not a fan of medication, prescription medication in particular but generally all medication, including aspirin, Advil, and so on. I have a deeply rooted belief, formed from watching my father's health challenges, that medications contribute to poor quality of life. Before I lost weight, my doctor was ready to recommend blood pressure and cholesterol medication. My compelling reason kept me on track.

Creative

This is where we get to have some fun. When we get creative, we can actually make our goals enjoyable. Continue to ask yourself better questions. Our minds work like Google: you ask great questions and you get great answers; when you ask poor questions, you get poor answers. For example, how can I lose weight and enjoy the process? If it is only about losing weight, I may settle for a salad every day and get bored with that. If I want to lose weight and *enjoy the process*, my mind is going to search for ways to enjoy it—add pumpkin seeds, different dressing, protein variety.

The second part of being creative is stretching the goal. Maybe your goal is to complete a project by the end of the month; a stretch would be to complete it two days early. Or maybe your goal is to increase revenue by $1 million; a stretch would be to expand that goal to $2 million.

Example: I want to lose ten pounds so that I can look good in a bathing suit *and enjoy myself in the process*. Ahh, we may find some more fun ways to lose weight with that qualifier on the end.

I love games, and if I do say so myself, I'm pretty good at them: card games, backgammon, bowling. My parents taught me how to play backgammon on the living room couch when I was seven years old. They loved to play in the evening with each other. I started by watching, then learning the rules, then the strategy, and then I grew into a decent player. For those unfamiliar with the game, it is a race to move your chips around the board to home base, and you pick them up based on the roll of two dice. The first player to pick up all their chips wins the game.

As I got older, I learned new strategies that fared well against older strategies. After all, this is a five-thousand-year-old game invented in Mesopotamia in the Middle East. My wife and I visited the Middle East, and when her uncle Gibran heard that I knew how to play backgammon, his eyes lit up. He had envisioned another sheep ready for the slaughter. He was fluent in Arabic with about ten words of English. I am fluent in English with about ten words of Arabic. Our common language was the game.

So, we set up and rolled the dice. I quickly observed that he played the way my parents had when I was just a kid. He moved his chips around the board keeping them safe along the way. If they were exposed, they risked getting sent back to the start. To be successful at backgammon, you need a combination of great skill and some luck since it involves rolling dice. I beat him the first game; he chalked it up to luck, and we set up for game two. I beat him again. He grew a bit more frustrated, and I started to wonder if this was the best way to endear myself to my wife's family. After three losses, Uncle Gibran had to wonder if this was all luck. And after five straight wins for the good guy, he said something in Arabic that I swear to this day was a curse on the future generations of my family.

Paul Magriel's 1976 book *Backgammon* says it well: "Although modern backgammon players are still interested in the basic aspects of the race, experts now understand that few games directly evolve into one. You need to rapidly mobilize your men and seize key points early in the game. A dynamic and aggressive style of play is demanded. You are willing to take chances of being hit—even in your inner board—if this enables you to move your men into an effective position quickly." In other words, a modern style of play involves taking risks.

Many times, taking appropriate risks will yield better results. These are not crazy risks; think of them as asymmetrical. "Asymmetrical risk" simply means taking a risk that will deliver results that outperform the amount of risk. An example of asymmetrical risk is an investment that has a better-than-average chance of earning an 8 percent return, and the risk of the investment losing value is close to zero.

As you're putting your roadmap together, be creative and be willing to take some risks that will yield significant positive results.

Calendared

To accomplish our goals, we must schedule time for them. First, set a target date for when the goal will be completed. Next, schedule time on your calendar to work on your goal. These two simple actions will make your goal concrete.

Example: I want to lose ten pounds *by June 30th* so that I can look good in a bikini and enjoy the process. To accomplish this goal, meal planning time, shopping time, meal preparation time, and exercise must also be scheduled.

When I set out to lose weight, my trainer said to me, "Don, you seem like you're a planner, is that right?"

Well, yes, for sure. Is this a trick question? I thought. "Yes," I said.

"Can you plan out your food for the week?"

"No idea."

"Okay, would you like to go food shopping together?"

"Are you asking me out on a date?" I laughed. In reality, I was thrilled with the offer. He showed me the importance of planning your meals and shopping if you are serious about losing weight. After that discussion, I blocked time on my calendar for shopping and meal preparation. More on how to do that in Chapter Ten.

Celebrated

As a good friend of mine reminds me, "If you want something to grow, pour champagne on it." Find a way to celebrate your goals. Celebrate them at three levels:

- Celebrate setting them.
- Celebrate the big milestones and the small milestones.
- Celebrate when they are complete.

When you celebrate your wins, you stay in the mindset of winning, of accomplishing your goals. Celebrating wins compels you to focus on accomplishments, which will breed more accomplishments.

Example: I had tried to lose weight several times before, and nothing seemed to work for me. The final, successful time (I've kept the weight off for years now), I observed the results along the way, which in itself is motivating; I made adjustments to stay on track; and I celebrated the small milestones. Then, when my health club recognized me as the member of the month when I lost twenty-five pounds, I had a bigger celebration.

CREATE YOUR ROADMAP   **73**

I'll admit, celebrating is not a strength of mine, but I do recognize the importance of it. Let's all strive to be better at celebrating the small and big milestones.

Communicated

Once you have a goal that is crystal, computable, compelling, creative, calendared, and celebrated, you are ready to share your goal with others. The advantage of making it public is that you will be more accountable about making it happen.

When I started writing this book, I was reluctant to share with others. What if I don't finish? What if it's not good? What if no one cares? My writing coach encouraged me to share the process with my followers. When I did that, two things happened. The first video I shared got thousands of views, and sharing became fun. The other thing that happened was that I knew I had to make it happen. Backing down at that point was not an option. One caveat to a communicated goal is that you want to share your goal with people you know will support you, not people who will get in the way.

Example: When I embarked on the weight-loss journey yet again, I told my trainer about it, of course, and also my wife, my parents, and my closest friends. They all supported me throughout my weight-loss journey.

Get moving! Go tell people about your goal.

PRODUCTIVITY CORNER
Khouri's Seven Cs

Let's have some fun with the Seven Cs. For each item on your roadmap, develop your goal using the Seven Cs. Before you move to the next chapter, please make sure you have completed your roadmap, with crystal clear goals for each component.

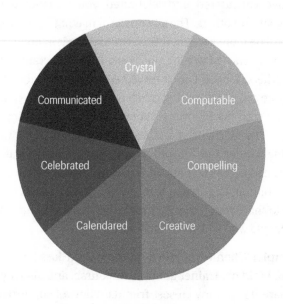

KEY PRODUCTIVITY POINTS

- When you have a clear roadmap, you'll be clearer about when to say yes.

- Utilize a new and improved goal-setting approach—Khouri's Seven Cs:

  - Crystal
  - Computable
  - Compelling
  - Creative
  - Calendared
  - Celebrated
  - Communicated

You can work independently and accomplish a great deal, you can work co-dependently relying on others, or you can work interdependently and depend on each other to get your goals accomplished.

DON KHOURI

Define Your Relationship Hierarchy

1
Create your
roadmap

2
Define your
relationship hierarchy

3
Assess the quality
of the request

4
Prioritize and
reprioritize

5
Master
delegation

YOU'RE ABOUT TO head out the door to what your boss told you is a career-changing meeting. You have just enough time to finish preparing yourself, get in the right mindset, and get to the meeting on time.

Your spouse says, "Honey, wait, could you hang this picture over the doorway? It will only take five minutes."

What do you do? You already have a standing commitment and now a new request from your spouse. Both requesters are important to you. In the first request, the requester is your boss and you want to advance. In the second request, it's your spouse, maybe the most important person in your life.

This is what I call the requester trade-off. Many would look at this situation and think, *This is easy. I can hang the picture anytime; the meeting is more important.* Others might think, *My spouse is the most important person in the world, and it will only take a couple of minutes.* Remember the planning fallacy. How many times have you started a home project thinking it would take a few minutes, and it took much longer? Maybe it's just me.

How do we make this decision? What if the request wasn't hanging a picture above the doorway? What if your spouse was sick, or what if he or she was not able to drop the kids off at school, or what if your mother-in-law had been rushed to the hospital? The stakes would be higher. Part of the decision to accept a request for your time involves assessing who is asking.

Who takes precedence? What I have learned from the most productive executives is that they possess a relationship hierarchy. The relationship hierarchy is a ranked list, with no duplicates, of the most important requesters in your life. In other words, you don't want to have three number-one relationships or two number-five relationships. Think of it as a flat list from one to n. For some, this ranking was conscious and clear. For others, it was more subconscious.

The Relationship Hierarchy

After you've built your roadmap, the second step is to define your relationship hierarchy. When we think about how we are connected to those who request our time, there are six types of relationships:

- Existing important relationships
- Existing relationships to foster
- New relationships that are important for your roadmap
- New relationships that may or may not fit into your roadmap
- Existing relationships where trust is high
- Existing relationships where trust is low

Existing relationships play a significant role in how we evaluate requests for our time. Some significant existing relationships are manager, spouse, family member, and customer. All of these relationships have some level of importance, and we will pay more attention to requests from these requesters.

To see the relationship hierarchy in action, let's return to the example of George Bailey. Part of the Bailey family plan was for George to lead the family business while his brother Harry went off to college. When Harry returned, he would take over the business so that George could go to college and follow through on his plan to travel and see the world. When Harry returns, however, he surprises the family (and George, of course) with a wife. Harry had married, and his father-in-law had offered him a plush job in his business. George has two choices: he can go off to college and let the family business, the Bailey Building and Loan, fail, or he can stay and support the business and clients. He chooses to stay and run the family business. George put the relationship with his brother, and to some degree his relationship with his deceased father, above his personal need to travel and go to college.

Later, George faces another choice when his friend, Sam Wainright, an executive at a plastics manufacturing company, asks him to take a job. George has two choices: move (travel) to take on the job, or stay in Bedford Falls to start a relationship with Mary and take care of his customers. Again, he puts his relationship with Mary and his family ahead of his need to travel, and he fights his initial resistance and makes a thoughtful, conscious decision.

George is asked to exercise his relationship hierarchy yet again when a rival, Mr. Potter, learns that George and the Bailey Building and Loan are doing well and cutting into Potter's business. Potter schemes to hire George and make him part of the company. He invites George into his office, hands him a fine cigar, and offers him a job at $20,000 ($250,000 in 2020), which is about ten times what George is making as a business owner. Potter also offers him the opportunity to travel on business trips to New York and Europe. To George, it sounds like a dream. George does not think about this opportunity for long, however, because he realizes that the relationship is not one that he wants to honor.

"I don't need twenty-four hours; I don't have to talk to anybody. I know right now, and the answer is no, no." We can

conclude from the movie that George prioritized his relationships in this way: his father (and the Bailey Building and Loan),
Mary, his children, his brother, Uncle Billy, and his friends
(such as Violet, Bert, and Ernie). Potter was nowhere on the list,
and as soon as George realized that, he knew how to respond
to Potter's job request.

The Mindset of the Most Productive People

Moving from fiction to reality, high-performing professionals
and executives often base their decisions on their own personal relationship hierarchies. Let me introduce you to Fred,
a CTO of an information company based in the Netherlands,
with local offices in Boston. He runs an organization of five
hundred people worldwide. He described it this way: "If [my
boss] comes to me and says, 'We've got a problem here. We
need to fix it '... I hop on it."

James, a CIO new in his role in a midsize financial services
company, had a similar approach: "If my boss sends [an email],
I'm gonna go to that first." For these two, their boss was at or
near the top of the relationship hierarchy.

Many of the leaders I spoke to said that reinforcing existing
relationships and building new relationships were important
when evaluating requests for their time. For instance, even
their response to my request for an interview was partially
influenced by our pre-existing relationship. When I asked how
they processed my request to participate, I received responses
such as "old buddy" and "name recognition."

Others discussed the importance of building new relationships. Robert, a CTO at an Ivy League educational institution,
asserted, "It is important to micromanage your first and
last impression." Sam, the CIO of a large financial services

company with over 2,500 information technology profession-als, agreed: "If it's relationship building and I know that'll help at some point, I'll invest there, too." I love how Sam thought about his time as an investment—"I'll invest there, too." He's not spending time, he's investing time. Investing is a different mindset from spending. Investing means that you will get a return—a better relationship, more time back in the end, or some other value as a result of the investment.

Trust is another important factor they considered. Robert, the education CTO, was clear about the importance of trust: "Trust allows for unfiltered communication." He went on to say, "You have to work very aggressively and very quickly to start to get those relationships in place. And then once you have those in place, then at least the ball will start moving. If you don't put those in place nothing happens... If there's any sense of distrust, you're just out. Period." If someone requests your time, do you already have a relationship of trust with that person? Does trust need to be built, or does this request present an opportunity to build trust? If you haven't built up trust with the requester, you will naturally give more thought to how to process the request.

Troy, senior vice president of application development and maintenance at a Boston company, shared an example of a request that came through email and was missing infor-mation. He felt he needed to gather more information before responding to the request because trust was missing from the relationship. If he had previously established trust with the requester, he may not have needed the additional information to accept the request.

The leaders I spoke with said they judge the value of the request against their relationship hierarchy. Once they deter-mine if the request belongs on their roadmap, they evaluate the requester. You may be thinking, *Isn't this really about*

Technology does not run an enterprise, relationships do.

PATRICIA FRIPP

priority? In a sense, you are correct, and it's all about priority ultimately. However, you will see in Chapter Six that priority is about evaluating the priority relative to everything else currently on your action list.

One of my executive coaching clients, Tim, who is the CTO in a Boston-based technology company, had a request from his boss, who was second on his relationship hierarchy, right behind customers. Tim's boss wanted him to attend a dinner with potential clients. He evaluated the request and determined its value did not outweigh what he already had planned for that evening. He respectfully declined.

Some leaders I spoke to place a high value on all relationships, and connecting with requesters is a welcome part of their work. James indicated a desire to be accessible for people: "I respect everyone when they make a request." Eric described his self-proclaimed core competency as working with other people: "I care a lot about people... when people have personal needs, I make that a priority. I've got to [get the work done] through others, right? [The project] went very well and everybody says it went well, but it's not based on my expert knowledge, it's based on my ability to work with people and find trade-offs. That has been more my MO than being a technical leader or organizational expert."

Other questions emerged about the contextual nature of the relationships in evaluating requests. For example, would the relationship hierarchy change for a request regarding a production outage versus a strategic request? Would the relationship hierarchy change if there was a family emergency? Would the relationship input matter differently if there was an apparent mismatch between the requester and the request? Part of your decision-making process will be to give the requester more or less weight than the priority. More on priorities in Chapter Six.

Although the people I spoke to had a different rank or order, most agreed that they had a relationship hierarchy that helped them make decisions, even if it was not always explicit.

My Own Hierarchy

Let me share my hierarchy with you. I am an entrepreneur and lead my own executive coaching business with a team of coaches serving executives and healthcare professionals. I have requests from clients, team members, coaching colleagues, vendors, alliance partners, and family members, and what follows is my explicit hierarchy.

Me. To be truly purposely productive, we have to put ourselves first. Say yes to yourself. If you take care of yourself, then you can take care of others. Put your own oxygen mask on first, so to speak. Start by saying yes to yourself when you wake up. I have a morning routine that I rely on to put me in the right mindset for the day. This includes breakfast, meditation, exercise, roadmap review, and powerful questions. I do this before I check social media or email.

I request time from myself, too. Time to write, time to work on a project, time to process incoming requests. I need to respect this time, and I block time on my calendar for it. I treat myself as a requester and place myself in the hierarchy. For example, I had time blocked on a Friday afternoon to prepare for the tax meeting with my CPA, but I got a request to support a client on a marketing initiative that same day. I was able to find another time to prepare for the meeting with the CPA and to service the client. On the other hand, I will not easily give up my evening time or morning routine time, unless there is a real emergency. If you plan ahead, many things can be scheduled at optimal times. This applies to bigger projects as well, such as starting a social media campaign, launching a podcast, updating your website, and reorganizing the department. Apply the same practice to a request you make of yourself.

First, capture the thought in your list of actions so that you don't lose track of it. If you don't do that, your brain will keep reminding you of it until you do something about it or decide not to, and that is a distraction. Does it align with your roadmap? I can almost guarantee requests from yourself fit on your relationship hierarchy. How could you make the quality of this request worth paying attention to? What priorities need to change to accommodate your new idea? The key difference is recognizing a request from yourself.

As I write this, I am thinking about launching a podcast. It certainly aligns with my roadmap because it will help me grow my business and I enjoy the format (video and audio). I'm not yet sure what would have to be deprioritized to give the podcast priority. I'm also not sure what time commitment would be required to make it successful. So, my next step is to talk to podcasting experts and learn more from them before I take it on.

PRODUCTIVITY CORNER
Set Your Mindset for the Day

Evaluate your current morning routine and consider incorporating all or some of these activities to put you in the right frame of mind to be purposely productive:

- Meditation

- Exercise

- Reviewing your mission statement, roadmap, goals

- Asking powerful questions like, What am I most grateful for in my life? What would a successful day look like? Who can I inspire today?

- Breath exercises

- Drinking water

Design a morning routine that will work for you, and block the time you need on your calendar with a recurring daily appointment.

Family. Family is important to me. When I look at scheduling my time, I schedule family time just like I do business time or other personal time. As I look ahead and plan my calendar, I block "me" time and family time first, because if I don't do that, it becomes much more difficult to schedule.

When you do receive a request from a family member, factor in how often you interact with them. If the interactions with the requester are frequent, you may not need to respond as quickly to the request, depending on the urgency. If the interactions are less frequent, you may need to pay more attention. For example, I speak with my wife every day. We know, based on the call or text, how urgent the request is. If the request is urgent enough, it will go to the top of the list. If it's not urgent, I can wait until the end of the day.

Clients. I had a client contact me about a bad review she had received on Yelp regarding her business. There was some urgency to her request because a timely response to the review was important. I contacted her at the next possible opportunity and asked if we could meet Friday morning. She was not available. Then I asked how long the meeting would take. "Thirty minutes," she said. Given that I already enjoyed a relationship of trust with the client and knew that she would honor the time limit, I was okay modifying my block by thirty minutes to accommodate her. Perhaps someone else would not be as respectful of time or not understand that time is one of my highest values.

Team members. If I take care of my team, they will take care of our clients. If I take care of the team, they will take care of me. I have often been praised for my responsiveness to the team. Seventy-four percent of employees want their managers to listen, understand, and respond.[1] That's one way to take care of them. Recently, as a team, we identified each team member's preferred way of being appreciated—some prefer acts of service, others words of affirmation, and others time. Or I may send a small motivation card or gift to let them know I care.

Coaching colleagues. If a colleague needs something, I support them. Zig Ziglar, one of the great motivational speakers, says, "You can have everything in life you want if you will just help enough other people get what they want."[2] Bernie Stoltz, the CEO of Fortune Management, the nation's leading and largest executive coaching firm for dentists, defines success this way: "Find out what people want, how they want it, and deliver it quickly and elegantly."[3]

The way this hierarchy works is this: if a colleague asks for something at the same time a client asks for something, I will likely prioritize the client. Clients are first, and colleagues are important and simply lower on the list.

Alliance partners. Alliance partners are others who also serve my clients. They are partners because we work together in the best interest of the client. In some cases, I refer clients to them. So I have a relationship with them, and these requesters will get my time, depending on the urgency of the request and how client-focused it is.

Vendors. Vendors get the lowest priority from me, as they did for the executives whom I spoke to during my study. We are inundated with vendor requests. It is much easier for us to say no to vendor requests. To be clear, that is not to say that these relationships are not important, but they are less urgent than other requests and relationships. Nevertheless, we depend on our vendors to deliver quality solutions.

THINK ABOUT someone you know who loves to party and is often the life of the party. That person likely places a high value on relationships. I'm not necessarily the life of the party, and as you can see, when it comes to my own productivity, I place a high value on relationships as well. Some leaders value relationships more than others. Some will make a decision to do business based on a relationship. Other leaders may place more importance on moving fast and getting things done, while still others will place more value on information than on relationships.

However, for everyone, and I do mean everyone (reading this book, at least), the relationship hierarchy is critical. In order to give all requests the attention they deserve, it's a simple reality that you have to rank them. The reason this is so important is that at the time of decision, this is one of the key factors that we must evaluate to protect our time. Am I going to prioritize this request coming in from Sue over the one that I already committed to from John? The trade-off can also come in the moment. One of the leaders I spoke with, Kevin, the CIO of an IT solutions provider in New Hampshire, was resolute that a call from his boss would warrant an interruption: "If I'm meeting with you right now and my boss calls, I'll say, 'Excuse me, I have to take this.'"

When You Make Requests

Where do you think you fall in other people's relationship hierarchies? In other words, if they were reading this book and enumerating their most important requesters, would you be on the list? Put another way, are the people whom you want to listen to you actually listening to you? If so, take a minute to document what is working. What's the reason they listen to you? What have you done over time to build that trust? How often and quickly do they accept your requests?

What about those you care about but who may not be listening to you? What's not working with that relationship? What can you do today to start turning that around? Is it about the requests, the relationship, or something else? What would help you make stronger cases to those who you care about the most—your spouse, your boss, your clients, your prospective clients? Just because it is not working now doesn't mean that you can't change it. Your requesters may or may not have read this book, and they may be taking these steps at a more subconscious level.

Here's an example of a situation where my requests were not being considered and I turned it around. One of the initiatives I proposed at Fidelity was outsourcing technical support activities to India. The need was clear. We were developing new software, and while we were doing that, we needed to keep the current system operational. The top developers wanted to work on the new system rather than maintain the existing system. This is a typical trade-off in software development. Teams want to work on the new technology, not the old. The opportunity was to outsource the old technology maintenance to a company in India. When I first approached my boss about this, he laughed at me. His perspective was that we had mission critical systems, and it would be careless to outsource that core skill set. What if something went wrong and we had to explain to executive management that our developer in India created that bug? It just wouldn't look good.

However, my request clearly aligned with the organization's roadmap—maintain the existing system and develop the replacement. I was somewhere on my manager's hierarchy. I had to take action to continue to build trust so that he would accept this request. I improved the plan, thought about contingencies, and created a phased approach. Ultimately, he accepted the request. The outsourcing in India continued to grow across the firm to include two prominent technology companies in Bangalore and Mumbai, as well as the establishment of our own captive organizations. Some called me the "father of India" at Fidelity, not because I was responsible for that growth, but because I was among the first to outsource critical support offshore.

PRODUCTIVITY CORNER
Develop a Relationship Hierarchy

Now it's your turn to build your own relationship hierarchy. You may have one that operates at a subconscious level, or maybe you've never given it any thought. In either case, the key to evaluating requests for your time is having a hierarchy, and here's how to do it:

1   List all of the requesters in your life. Write down the name of everyone who has or may make a request of your time.

2   List the categories of requester (e.g., "Client," "Family," "Boss," and so on).

3   Place each requester into a category.

4   Rank the categories.

5   Rank the names within each category.

6   List where you believe you fall on hierarchies for those who are important to you.

KEY PRODUCTIVITY POINTS

- We receive requests from many different types of requesters, like family, clients, team, and vendors.

- It is important to identify a relative hierarchy of these requesters to remain purposely productive.

- Your morning routine puts you in a mindset that will set the tone for your day.

- Evaluate how people in valued relationships with you respond to your requests. Are you getting the results you want?

If you don't have the confidence
to ask, you will never have the
confidence to convince.

AMIT KALANTRI

Assess the Quality of the Request

1

Create your
roadmap

2

Define your
relationship hierarchy

3

Assess the quality
of the request

4

Prioritize and
reprioritize

5

Master
delegation

I HEARD A STORY about Harry Truman. I'm not sure if it is true or not, but it will serve to make a point. Harry Truman, the thirty-third president of the United States, asked his cabinet to prepare a recommendation on a Monday morning. They said, "Absolutely, Mr. President. Give us a couple of days, and we will have that ready for you."

President Truman's cabinet came back Friday afternoon and plopped it on his desk. He took it with him for the weekend and came back the next Monday morning. He asked, "Is this absolutely the best you can do?"

"Well, we could probably beef up section two and be more compelling in section number four," they said. They worked on it all week and brought it back to President Truman that next Friday afternoon.

He took it with him for the weekend. On the following Monday morning, he asked, "Is this absolutely the best you can do?"

The cabinet members responded, "Well, we could probably have more data to support our points and more graphs in the last section." They worked on it all week and brought it back the next Friday afternoon. This time they were proactive and said, "Before you ask, this is absolutely the best we can do, we have all our data, covered all our bases. This is the best report."

President Truman said, "Great, now I'll read it."

The most productive people expect requests for their time to be thought through and crystal clear; otherwise, they will refuse the request.

Five Components of a Quality Request

What does a quality request for your time look like?

There is a theory called speech act theory, first introduced by J. L. Austin in 1962 in his book, *How to Do Things with Words*. A speech act is an action expressed in speech, such as, "Can you pass the asparagus?" or a request like, "I'd like you to take on project ABC." The action is what the requester expects of the listener. The requester intends to affect the behavior of the listener by making the request. The language in the request is important. The participants in my study did not know about speech act theory, but what they did know is that the way a request was made influenced whether they would accept the request or reject it.

A quality request has five components:

1 **It is respectful of your time.** A quality request sounds like, "Is this a good time to talk?" or, "Can we schedule a time to talk about project ABC?" It is respectful of the responder's time and accounts for the medium of communication: email, face-to-face, or phone call. The richer the request, the more important it is to use a higher form of connection or communication. Simple requests can be made in an email; more complicated, and you may need to contact the person by phone. For even more complex or sensitive requests, set up face-to-face time.

I was recently thinking about changing my rate structure with a long-time client from a legacy hourly rate to a monthly rate. In fact, I was not charging by the hour anymore. So, that needed to be a face-to-face discussion. It was somewhat sensitive and required me to read all body language, tone of voice, and any other factors to respond in the appropriate ways. Remember, it is much more difficult to communicate tone in email. It's not impossible, just much more difficult. For requests over text message, we want to keep it limited to simple, everyday-type requests to your closest friends and colleagues.

2   **It is necessary.** The requester has considered the request in the larger context of what is important. Make sure you are clear on what's in it for the receiver. Why is this request important to them? How will it benefit the company? How will it benefit the customer? The requester has a sense of the time and resources it will take to process and execute the request; they know the importance of this request relative to other priorities. Also, consider the responder's communication style by answering the following questions: Do they want quick and to the point? Then give them what they need and move on. Make it fast. Do they desire a relationship? Do they prefer big picture or details? Do they need lots of information? Do you expect them to have questions? Do you need to take your time? Do they thrive on change or resist change? This is not a communication book or an influence book. This chapter is about deciding whether the requests made for your time and requests that you make of others are necessary.

3   **It is well thought out.** The requester knows exactly what they are requesting, and their request is to do something, approve something, or brainstorm. If the requester is there only to chat and is not clear about what they want, it is not a quality request.

The most
productive
people expect
requests for
their time
to be thought
through.

4 **It is clear and concise.** The requester communicates the request in an efficient way. If the requester is rambling in person or in email, they have not completely thought through how to make the request. One of the leaders I spoke to said, "I find an email that's longer than a certain duration is automatically going to delay [me]... if you need more than a paragraph to explain a problem in an email, we need a meeting or you are weak in your ability to explain it."

5 **It includes solutions.** If we are bringing a problem or challenge or opportunity, we must also bring solutions with it. I suggest to my executive coaching clients that they bring three solutions for every problem, challenge, or opportunity when asking for help. Remember, we want to let the responder know that we have planned this and thought through the entire process. So, in a quality request, the requester brings options and a solution. The request sounds like, "Here's the problem/challenge/opportunity, here are the options we have, and here's what I recommend."

Taking this list into account, have you been considering low-quality requests for your time?

The Problem with Low-Quality Requests

During the trip to the Middle East I mentioned earlier, when I beat Uncle Gibran in backgammon, we visited the city my mother-in-law is from. It's a four-thousand-year-old city, and when we arrived after a two-hour drive, I was ready to sit and relax and meet her family. Driving in the Middle East is not like driving in the US or Europe. Although there are some highways, most are smaller roads that are not maintained as well as our roads in the US. So, it's not as smooth a ride.

When we arrived, twenty-five family members were there and ready to welcome us. We greeted everyone and then sat around in a large living room. People were speaking mostly in Arabic, and I understood very little. After a few minutes, the crowd thinned to maybe fifteen, then ten, then five people. Soon, I was in the room alone wondering if I had said something inappropriate.

My wife's aunt finally came back into the room and said, "Come on," which loosely translated from the Arabic can mean, "Come and eat."

I thought, *Well, I'm not that hungry, but let's see what they have.* Middle Eastern food is always a favorite.

But she was actually saying, "Come on." I didn't see any food. Everyone was outside, in a caravan of cars, ready for another trip. They had all decided it would be nice to show me the Roman ruins a short drive away.

"How long is the drive?" I asked, still recovering from the two-hour bumpy ride up.

"Oh, it's a short drive."

"I understand. Approximately how long?"

"About fifteen minutes."

"Okay great, I'm in."

So, we drove and drove and drove. Another two hours. Yikes, I was ready to lose my lunch at this point. When we arrived, we learned that the outdoor museum was closed. I would have been happy sitting on the couch socializing with the family.

Three key learning points emerge from this story. First, making a request of someone takes planning and thought. In my example, the requesters had the best of intentions. They wanted me to be entertained and see a place that was exciting to them. A little planning ahead of time would have accounted for travel time and closing time, and the request would have been a lot clearer.

Second, if you do receive a request that lacks clarity, you can respectfully bounce it back to the requester so they can provide that clarity. Or you can seek clarification until you do understand the request. The latter takes more time and effort on your part.

Third, a requester will be more successful soliciting your time if they know what is important to you. They could have known that all that was important to me at that point was to relax and enjoy my new friends.

Keep this in mind when you request other people's time. If you are going to influence someone, you need to know what influences them.

An Example of a Quality Request

To drive home the importance of quality requests, let's revisit George Bailey's example again. When his father passes away, George is faced with an important choice. He can either go on his planned trip with bag in hand or he can stay and take over his father's business. The request comes from the board of directors of the business, which has met to review the options and decided that unless George takes over, they will sell to Mr. Potter, the richest man in town.

First, the board of directors is respectful of George's time. They invite him to a preplanned meeting and give him the opportunity to present his case for the fate of the Bailey Building and Loan. They also know what is important to George: "I think that's all we'll need you for, George. I know you are anxious to make your train."

Second, the request is necessary. A decision needs to be made about the Building and Loan, and they need George's input, since he's been running the show since his father's death: "Now we come to the real purpose of the meeting: to appoint a successor to our dear friend, Peter Bailey."

Third, it is well thought out. Potter, who sits on the board, wants to dissolve the Building and Loan, or they would need to hire someone else to run it. However, after considering all the options, the board determined that keeping the business open and asking George to lead it was the best solution: "George, George, they voted Potter down, they want to keep it going. They've got one condition, only one condition... they've appointed [you] as executive secretary to take [your] father's place."

Fourth, it is clear and concise: "They'll vote with Potter otherwise."

Fifth, it includes solutions. They offer a solution for keeping the Building and Loan operational. George serves as executive secretary; otherwise, they dissolve the Building and Loan, as Potter wants.

This is a quality request. It is thoughtful, well planned, and made in a way so that George's options are clear. However, the request to take over his father's business does not align with George's roadmap, so he must make a trade-off. Ultimately, George decides to take over the business for many reasons, not the least of which is that the request was made in a quality way. If this had been a haphazard request, or one made in passing without much thought or planning, George may not have accepted the request.

The Mindset of the Most Productive People

In order to better understand the type of request we expect to receive, let's consider the requests that we make of other people. We need to apply the same rigor to our own requests as we demand of others. How do we get the attention of the people we want in a busy world? Adam shared that he personally had to be more specific in his requests and not assume that the other person understood the request: "I had to become more specific in my ask, at least from the new [team] members, but I use it for everything and everyone now. I had to change to be more specific in my demands to others, and [for] some things just spelling [it] out rather than just assuming the other person will get it."

The senior leaders I spoke to said that because they valued their time, they wanted the requests that came to them to be well thought through.

Leila was clear that action items needed to be in email rather than through other electronic tools: "[Instant messaging] is really just for conversations. I don't really look at it for things with action items, and conversely email is not appropriate for conversations... I want all that useless chatter that goes around in the email system out of email and [to] get that in instant messaging." Walter, an independent CIO, supported this notion as well: "I see [text and instant messaging] as [a] kind of conversation. It shouldn't be action that they want me to take..."

Robert said that he'd wait for a requester to make the request at least twice, sometimes three times, because the need often goes away. "Everybody thinks something is important when they hear about it, but it may not be that important. So, if you let them cool down, more than half the time the need actually goes away. If you can, push it out... and then let it just go away—again, unless it's something really of high value." Luckily, I had the foresight to make my request to Robert to participate in the study more than once. He responded the second time.

Luke said he'd refuse a request that did not have multiple options and a recommended solution; he'd also refuse it if he lacked a rapport with the requester or did not have confidence that the requester had planned out the request:

I refuse requests for my time for various reasons... [The request] wasn't fully thought through. I didn't like the vendors. When somebody wants some of my time, I need to have choices, okay? Somebody needs to give me an alternative as well as a main solution. [If] somebody just gives me a solution, I tend to pick that apart and [think] they haven't done their homework... I've got to believe that they planned this out. Otherwise, I will refuse them my time. I tell them to go away and come back better prepared.

Fred put a system in place to handle all the requests he received, and as a result, requests decreased significantly: "You put your request in and you need to define what it is, and then if it looks like it makes sense, you need to put your business case together. My requests went down 90 percent." Conversely, James's approach was to be accessible: "If someone wants my time in the company, I'll try to [be] available. It could be speaking at a division meeting, it could be [that] someone says, hey, I'd love you to meet so and so—I would do that. I want to be accessible; it's really important."

Eric grouped the quality of the request with the relationship factor: "I deal more to relationship. It's a little less hard and fast—it is [based] more on a relationship. Depending on who it is and how people ask, and how well I know the folks— that's one way to get their stuff prioritized."

PRODUCTIVITY CORNER
Assess and Make Requests

I invite you now to take action to lock in what you have learned in this chapter.

1   Review a request for your time that you received in email. Match up the request to the five criteria outlined in this chapter and repeated below. Decide whether it meets the request quality you expect. If it does not, how would you change it so that it does?

2   Make sure all of your requests of other people are quality requests by using the following checklist:

- It is respectful of the other person's time.

- The responder will be able to see how it fits into the bigger picture and can articulate its importance.

- It is well thought out.

- It is crystal clear and concise.

- It includes solutions and a recommendation.

3   Consider how you would change the request quality criteria to fit your situation.

KEY PRODUCTIVITY POINTS

- There are five components of a quality request:
    - It is respectful of your time.
    - It is necessary.
    - It is well thought out.
    - It is clear and concise.
    - It has solutions.

The key is not to prioritize what's on your schedule, but to schedule your priorities.

STEPHEN COVEY

6

Prioritize and Reprioritize

1

Create your
roadmap

2

Define your
relationship hierarchy

3

Assess the quality
of the request

4

Prioritize and
reprioritize

5

Master
delegation

N 1998, my wife and I moved to Bedford, Massachusetts, the small town sandwiched between Lexington and Concord, of Revolutionary War fame. One of the reasons we moved there was that the fifty-four homes were built on fifty-eight acres of land *on* a golf course, a nine-hole PGA-rated golf course. We have a beautiful view of the sixth green from the back of our home. When I moved here, I loved to golf. I loved the peacefulness of the course, I loved the challenge, and I loved taking that perfect shot—you know, the one that brings you back every time.

And as much as I loved golf, I was never good at it. Just to give you a sense of my skill, one time I was golfing with my cousin Scott, a scratch golfer. That means he is really, really good. Halfway through the round, while making the turn from the ninth hole to the tenth hole, I asked him, "Scott, what do you think of my game?"

"It's not bad, Don," he replied. And then after a short pause he added, "But I prefer golf."

Independent of that encouragement, over time I struggled to spend four hours on a golf course on Saturday morning. Do I golf or spend time with my wife, who was taking care of her business all week? Do I go to the driving range or do some writing? Do I practice putting or exercise? Do I golf or rest? Over time, I made less time for golf.

When my golfing buddies asked me for a tee time, I would say, "I don't have time for golf."

When they asked, "Don, do you want to golf this weekend?" I'd say, "I don't have time."

"Don, we're planning a getaway weekend at a golfing resort. Are you in?"

"I don't have time."

What I was actually saying was, "It is not my *priority*." We find time for our priorities. Please remember this equation:

I do not have time = It is not a priority

Time is like a sponge; it absorbs what is important to you. In other words, we find time for what is important to us. Think about a time when you had an emergency. You deprioritized everything else so you could focus on that.

When my seventy-five-year-old father was exhibiting very unusual behavior, I paid attention. Normally, he was the most mild-mannered, easy-going gentleman you could ever meet. This time it seemed as if he had lost his judgment; he was getting upset at the smallest things. He was also exhibiting some unusual facial expressions, body movement, and body pain. We visited several doctors before arriving at a correct diagnosis. To help my dad figure out this diagnosis, I rearranged my schedule and other priorities. We find time for what's important.

What are your priorities? This is a key question, since even executives can suffer a serious mismatch between their priorities and how they allocate their time. A survey of 1,400 senior executives found that only *nine* percent said they were "very satisfied" with the relationship between how they used their time and what they hoped to accomplish. In addition, almost one-third said they were dissatisfied to some extent with how they used their time.[1]

Setting your priorities will help you make better decisions more quickly. The process has two dimensions:

1   Deciding what to do = value (What is most important?)

2   Deciding what to do first = time (What is most important now?)[2]

When you know your priorities, you'll know when to say yes, and you'll have an easier time saying no. Responding to a request by saying no may be perceived by others in a negative way, but "no" is the button that keeps us focused on our priorities. Saying it allows us to be productive.[3]

Priorities Come First

In *Getting Things Done,* David Allen offers a framework for deciding which action to focus on next. He asks people to consider four things in the following order:

1   Context (e.g., computer, phone, home)
2   Time available
3   Energy level
4   Priority

I appreciate Allen's work and learned a great deal from him in my early career. His Getting Things Done (GTD) methodology, which I learned in the 1989 MAP seminar mentioned earlier, gave me the freedom to be in the moment when I needed to be. In the second decade of the twenty-first century, however, I would reorder these criteria to put "priority" first.

If you don't prioritize your life, someone else will.

GREG MCKEOWN

Priority should drive context. Priority should drive time. Priority should also drive our energy levels. We all have the capability to adjust our energy level when we need to.

The ability to set priorities is critical to building a consistent record of achievement. Without a list of priorities, you won't know what to focus on, and this can cause you to miss important commitments, leading to compromised credibility. If you have ever felt overwhelmed by too much to do or unsure of where to focus, you likely need to improve your priority-setting skills as part of the Five Steps to Protect Your Time.

It is easier to make these decisions in the moment when your priorities are clear at the outset. It is easier to decide which urgent activities are truly important and which ones can be deferred. Think about your most important priority like this: You are in the elevator, and the CEO gets on the elevator and asks you, "What are you solving today?" This is a conversation starter that will force you to think about what you are going to get finished today. What is most important?

One C-level executive rationalized, "My job is to influence the six hundred business units... the role of the leader is to ask the folks that work for you, 'What's your priority? What are you working on now?'" Another leader explained that you have to organize your priorities in smaller chunks of time to be effective. He also reasoned that it is important for him to understand the multimillion-dollar projects and make the time necessary to get them done, which makes them a high priority.

So how do we ensure that our priorities come first and don't get lost in the rush and chaos of our fast-paced lives today? Effective priority setting includes focusing on the reason for doing something. When the reason is clear and compelling, you can use it to get back on track if you've been knocked off. When it's absent, it is much easier to get distracted. Your priorities need to be aligned with those of your company or organization, and if you're an executive or leader, you should be actively involved in setting effective priorities for your organization.[4]

The Mindset of the Most Productive People

Let's break this down even further and explore how high performers prioritize. Each time you contemplate a request for your time, you need to decide where the request fits in your priority list. Think about your time as an investment much like you would money in your investment portfolio. When you want to make a new purchase, say a particular stock, you may need to make room in your portfolio by selling something else. The same is true for your time. When you want to make room for a new project (one that will move you closer to your vision), you may need to say no to something else. This decision may currently be conscious or unconscious, and I'll show you how to make it conscious every time.

When I studied the behavior of high performers using a forty-six-item assessment with high reliability and validity that measures time management acumen, there were some interesting findings. All participants in my study completed it, and I discovered that most agreed with the statement, "I finish top-priority tasks before going on to less important ones," which scored an average of 4.0 on a scale of 1 to 5. Let's take a closer look at the seven factors they considered to determine priority: size, time, urgency, prior commitments, audit/regulatory requests, client requests/customer satisfaction, and production outages. Sometimes, one category is enough to drive priority, sometimes more than one will drive, and sometimes it will be all seven.

Size. High-performing leaders said they consider the size of the request to determine where it would fit on their list given the nature and size of their other commitments. Valerie, a program manager in a financial services firm, shared an example of a request made of her to run an agile boot camp (agile is a software development methodology), which involved inviting people from seven sites to Boston to give them an opportunity to form a community. The time frame was short. She said, "The first thing I did was [speak] with the woman who had done it before to get a sense of just the sheer size and complexity of the work, and also leverage any materials that she had already created. The hard thing is... that when you have something big... the little stuff keeps coming in."

Time. They also consider the time available to satisfy the request. One CIO who had been in his role for approximately three months blocked big chunks of time to focus on the most important priorities. "A good example is a big strategic project going on. I've had to do day-long deep dives to figure out what's going on. Those take a lot of time."

Urgency. What is the relative urgency of the request? "Is it a life-or-death thing?" Dawn, the CIO of a healthcare technology company, reflected on a request coming via email. "I think about the nature of the request, the requester, the urgency, the time to be able to complete the request, what [is] the intent or objective of the requesters—like, is there an agenda behind the request, to be blunt. In other words, what's the request and what's the meaning of the request, because the two might be different."

Tom, the chief innovation and technology officer of a mobile development services company, processed requests in a similar way: "It's valuable to do some analysis on it before responding, simply to know if everything was given to me [that I'll need] to even evaluate the request, and then if it's timely or there is an urgency to it, I'll obviously just jump in and start it."

Prior commitments. What happens when you have two competing priorities? The leaders I spoke to put a high value on meeting prior commitments. The commitment participants made to meet with me surfaced in more than one conversation. Something else may have surfaced that they determined was more important, yet they honored the commitment to me. One CIO left a budget meeting with his peers and manager to make sure he honored his commitment to give me an interview.

Luke, a tech CEO from Melbourne, shared an example of competing demands in light of a prior commitment, acknowledging that sometimes there is no one clear answer and you need to make a decision:

> I had that competing issue where [there was] a commercial commitment to meet a particular date. Days or hours beforehand, we found a massive bug that was related to another customer. What the hell do I do? Do I delay or try to get an extension or offer an olive branch? There's always that dilemma. I'll make a particular [decision] or I need to allocate more resources or I need to do a number of other things, but [it's] not pleasant.

Audit and regulatory requests. Many of the participants I interviewed work in the financial services industry, and many had a rule that a request from the audit department or a regulatory body took priority over other requests and warranted immediate attention.

Troy confirmed that there is little choice in accepting a request from the audit department: "Audit, I can schedule with them, but if we have to answer within a certain time and certain day... usually we have three days to answer. I cannot take two days or five days to answer. There were findings that said people broke the rules. I got a report just saying, 'Two of your guys accessed production and they are not supposed to'—just an example of that. So, immediately we have to explain why."

Eric also supported this idea of a request that you have to accept: "It happens all the time... I'll be asked to present at the audit committee meeting next Tuesday at four p.m. You know it is like a trump card—it trumps everything else. Other things have to be re-juggled. They're the ones that you don't really have a whole lot of choice in."

Client requests and customer satisfaction. Many of the executives I spoke to prioritized customer satisfaction at or near the top of requests. Luke put a high priority on "customer intimacy." By this he meant the relationship with the customer. He went on to say, "I take personal interest in providing access to my time and energy, ensuring that we do have very high customer satisfaction." For him, customer satisfaction was the second most important criteria, behind only honoring the date. Walter, the independent CIO, said of customer satisfaction that "the customer is the first to come to mind." James said customer satisfaction was equivalent to requests pertaining to a business problem or production outage.

Dawn was clear about the importance of customer service: "I would say any [requests] that come from my customers, I have to provide a level of customer service to them... There [are] requests from customers that say, 'This is an emergency, I need this executed today,' and it's something I have to engage [with]."

Fred agreed as well: "If it was something that was business-critical like client-facing stuff, that would be my first choice. I'd take care of that, and even if the request was client-facing versus my boss coming in for a request, I'd say to him, 'We have a real problem right now with this client. Let me get back to you.' Then people understand that."

Production outages. Any outage that affects customers or production systems usually warrants immediate attention. James evaluated production problems as a simple request:

> You need to make a decision what to do, because we're running an operation. It is a do-I-go-left or do-I-go-right... I quickly will get the facts, get the experts together, understand the situation, understand what do we think the options are, and then I might go and ask for more information, or I might make a decision as to what direction we need to go. A very iterative process, but time is of the essence.

Kevin was clear: "Any time a system is down, that's number one." Leila supported this notion as well: "In technology there's always the opportunity for something not to go as planned or there being an outage. If there's an outage, it affects everybody."

As you move into the next section to compose your priority list, consider each of these categories: size, time, urgency, prior commitments, audit and regulatory requests, client requests and customer satisfaction, and production outages. Everyone is different, and I encourage you to consider how the categories could be prioritized for you. This next exercise will help you determine exactly that.

PRODUCTIVITY CORNER
Compose a Priority List

Setting priorities is fun, and you will master it once the tools and tricks presented in this chapter become second nature.

The first thing you need to tackle is building your priority list. Based on what you've learned so far about how the most productive people set priorities, do the following:

Step 1   List all of your current commitments.

Step 2   Rank them.

Step 3   Write the amount of time you believe it will take you to complete each item on the list.

Step 4   For each item, assign a value of A if it is moving you closer to your vision or B if it is taking you away from focus on your vision.

Step 5   Schedule time in your calendar to focus on priorities 1, 2, and 3.

How to Reprioritize

If you're a football fan, you may know that an audible is used when the team's offense changes the play at the line of scrimmage based on the defensive formation. When the offense lines up, the quarterback looks at how the defense is lined up. He then calls the new play, hence the term "audible." He may signal a receiver or running back to move and then observe the defense's reaction. He then has to decide if the play that has been called is likely to work against the defense he is anticipating. If the matchups don't look favorable, he will call an audible.

Leaders do their homework and adjust their priorities; they know their values, they know what is most important, and they can align requests appropriately. One executive I spoke with said he asks himself the following: "How important is this request compared to the other requests coming in and everything else already on my plate?... The ability to juggle priorities is critical."

A subject in a similar study agreed: "The single biggest factor contributing to my success compared to others is the ability to juggle and prioritize all the information that is constantly coming toward me. I never let people hang on too long, and I always get things done. But I don't juggle by using technology; it is more of a mental balancing act and way of being than anything else." Another high performer from that study added, "The thing that sets me apart from others is that I constantly keep on top of, and reshuffle, what I need to do. As information comes to me, I keep it organized (in my head, through keeping my pending email list short, and a paper to-do list) so that I am sure to act proactively, not reactively."[5]

As these testimonials attest, it's important to reprioritize often and consistently. We live in a world of changing demands and priorities. To deal with priorities effectively, we must process incoming information, make sense of it, and decide if our current set of priorities needs to change or if we should stay the course. When I worked in the corporate world, the most effective leaders who worked for me were the ones who responded to one of my requests with, "Happy to do that, Don. Where does it fit on my priority list?"

Another question that comes up often is, "How do I handle two critical, simultaneous requests?" Here's what I heard from leaders on that topic. Think about the relative priority of each and then decide based on

- urgency;

- importance; and

- risk to the business and downstream implications if one of them were not to get done that day.

Notice that making the decision is key. Weigh the urgency, importance, and risk and decide.

Priorities are relative, not absolute. In other words, when a new request comes in, weigh it against the other priorities already on your list. How do you do this? Let's say you have a list of ten priorities and a new request comes in. Ask yourself two questions:

1   Is it a higher priority than project A, is it higher than project B, is it higher than project C, etc.? Keep going until you get a yes. If you don't get to a yes, refuse the request. This is intuitive, it takes only a few seconds, and it will save you time in the long run.

2   When does it need to be complete? Ask your requester for the deadline. Perhaps it is in a week or a month and does not need immediate attention. Postpone whenever possible.

To see how this works in practice, let's return to *It's a Wonderful Life*. On the day George and Mary are getting ready to leave for their honeymoon—yet another chance for George to travel—they experience torrential rain.

George is excited about finally getting to travel: "A whole week in New York. A whole week in Bermuda. The highest hotels. The oldest champagne. The richest caviar. The hottest music, and the prettiest wife." But just as they're leaving, they see a crowd outside the Building and Loan. Ernie, the taxi driver, says, "I've never really seen one, but that's got all the earmarks of being a run." In other words, people were trying to get their cash from the bank out of fear that the money would not be there.

George has an important decision to make: does he follow his passion to travel and honor the honeymoon with his wife, or does he investigate what's going on with the assembly of people outside his business? Mary pleads with him to stay the course with their travel plans.

Well, by now, I think you know George well enough to know that he gets out of the car and rushes, without an umbrella, to see what's going on. Many of the Five Steps to Protect Your Time are at play in this decision: he acts in accordance with his roadmap, his relationship hierarchy (Mary asking him not to get out of the car), and his priorities (he was already committed to something else). In this instance, George faced the equivalent of a production problem. The request was something that took priority over everything else. It was so urgent he deferred his travel plans again, and it trumped his wife's request (high on his relationship hierarchy).

George faces one more production-related request for his time, the sixth and final request in *It's a Wonderful Life*. This important event occurs on Christmas Eve, about halfway through the movie. George's uncle Billy, his business partner, misplaces $8,000 (the equivalent of $100,000 in 2020). As the audience, we know that Uncle Billy accidentally handed the money to Mr. Potter when he gave him back his newspaper at the bank on his way to making a deposit. George had big plans for the day because his brother was coming back from Washington, DC, after being recognized by the president as a war hero. However, he drops everything to retrace Uncle Billy's steps and find the money. It's the highest priority at the moment. Everything else drops down his priority list.

What is your production problem? If you are not a CTO or CIO who would prioritize that over anything else, there is something in your world that you would prioritize over almost everything else. What is it?

To deal with priorities effectively, we must process incoming information, make sense of it, and decide if our current set of priorities needs to change or if we should stay the course.

The Eisenhower Matrix

With a large volume of requests knocking on our metaphorical doors all day long, we need to triage and evaluate the priority of each one. Another tool you can use to help you navigate the immediate need to decide what to do and what to do first is the Eisenhower matrix, popularized by Stephen Covey's books *The Seven Habits of Highly Effective People* and *First Things First*.

Here's what the matrix looks like:

	URGENT	NOT URGENT
IMPORTANT	Do these first	Plan and schedule
NOT IMPORTANT	Delegate Reduce significantly	Does it need to be done?

Urgent and Important. We must pay attention to urgent and important requests now. If we don't, they will create bigger issues. An example of an urgent and important item is a fire, real or metaphorical. If you have a real fire, you drop everything else, get your loved ones, and get out. Nothing else is more important at that moment.

One time, I was getting ready to golf, and I took off my wedding ring and put it in my right pocket. When you golf, the wedding ring can impact your grip, so it was a common practice for me to take it off. When I got to the seventh hole, I realized that my wedding ring was not in my pocket. I distinctly remembered putting it in my right pocket. I checked my left pocket, my back pockets, my shirt pocket, and the pockets in my golf bag. It was nowhere. *I had lost my wedding ring!* That was when panic set in, because there was absolutely no way I was going to find a wedding ring on a golf course. What would I tell my wife? She'd understand, wouldn't she? No, she wouldn't. Did this mean we'd get a divorce? Could I get a replacement ring without her ever noticing?

Losing my wedding ring was a fire. It grabbed my focus and became *the* priority. So, I decided to try to find the ring. It was a long shot, but I had to give it a go. I retraced my steps, back to hole six, hole five, hole four. Anywhere I had taken a shot, I stopped to look. Nothing. Hole three, hole two, nothing. And then, just off the second tee, where I'd likely pulled the glove out of my pocket to put it on, *there it was*. I found it. Talk about relief. And I still have it today securely on my finger.

The point is that sometimes urgent and important items will require us to change our priorities. The secret, however, is minimizing the number of requests that fall into the "urgent" bucket.

Urgent and Not Important. If the request is urgent and not important, you can defer it, or it's an opportunity to delegate, which we'll talk more about in the next chapter. What you need to recognize is that not all urgent requests are important. Not all phone calls are important. Not all Facebook notifications are important. Not all text messages are important. Sometimes, we think they are because our devices are buzzing or dinging. The request seems important, but we don't know if it is.

How do we know if something is urgent or not? The first thing you can do is not process the request immediately. If something is actually that urgent and important, the requester will find a way to find you. Remember your phone is there for *you*, not the requester. Something else I strongly suggest is turning off notifications so you're not tempted to be distracted. When you are working on your goals, turn off your computer notifications and your phone notifications.

Important and Not Urgent. These items are planning activities. They are not requests at all. They are activities that you decide need to be done—for example, exercise, sleep, planning, working *on* your business (not *in* your business), visioning, and team building. What would you put into this quadrant? The more time you spend here, the less time you will be forced to spend on urgent and important items.

Have you ever had a time when something became urgent, and you realized you could have avoided it if you'd planned ahead? If you do not pay your electric bill for three months and the electric company is ready to turn off your electricity, this is urgent. If you pay your bill on time, it's important but not urgent. If you work with your team on team agreements and guiding principles, you may avoid the team conflict that arises because team members are not clear on how they are going to work together. Plan. Think. Focus.

Not Important and Not Urgent. If a request falls into this category, does it need to be done at all? What types of requests or activities fall into this category? Emails that your program moves to the junk folder, watching TV, or playing a game on your phone. When you assess the request, you may decide that it is not urgent but important. For example, if the request to watch TV comes from your family, not yourself, you may have set family time as a priority and will deem it important.

KEY PRODUCTIVITY POINTS

- When deciding what to focus on, priorities absolutely, positively, without a measure of doubt come first.

- When you get a new request for your time, think what needs to be reprioritized. In other words, don't accept more on your already full plate.

- Consider the following factors when reprioritizing:

  - size
  - time
  - urgency
  - prior commitments
  - audit/regulatory requests
  - client requests/customer satisfaction
  - production problems or outages

- Always consider the urgency and importance independently of the request for your time.

- Not enough time = not a priority.

No man will make a great business who wants to do it all himself or get all the credit for doing it.

ANDREW CARNEGIE

7

Master Delegation

1
Create your
roadmap

2
Define your
relationship hierarchy

3
Assess the quality
of the request

4
Prioritize and
reprioritize

5
Master
delegation

WHEN THE MOST productive executives consider a request for their time, they think about whether the job or task can be delegated. This is a critical step because although the request may meet the first four steps to protect your time, the leader still may not be the best person to take it on. Delegation can be a great strategy to allow you to stay focused on the roadmap while providing a growth opportunity for others. So, ask yourself, "Am I the only person who can do this?" If the answer is yes, then accept the request. If the answer is no, then consider whom to pass it to.

What's the purpose of delegating? Delegation helps us realize the goals on our roadmap. We delegate so that we can execute higher-priority work. We also delegate so that someone else can own a project instead of us—take it from beginning to end and own it, with our support. We also delegate as a development opportunity for someone else on the team.

When I started my coaching and training business in 2009, I did all the administrative and bookkeeping work myself. I could because I had the time. After a short time, I realized that administrative and bookkeeping tasks were taking me away from business development—and, more importantly, serving clients. So, I hired an administrative assistant who handled event planning, travel needs, and scheduling, among other items. Shortly after that, I hired a bookkeeper. Remember, anything that you are not the only qualified person to do, you can consider delegating. In fact, what if we focused on the work that we love to do, and that only we can do, and delegated the rest? We would be energized and charged at the end of the day, and purposely productive.

The Mindset of the Most Productive People

When I spoke with successful executives such as Luke, the CEO of a tech company, they stressed the importance of delegation: "I can delegate to someone I can trust and we work really well together... that's what works well for me. If [there's not someone like that in the] organization, I would be grooming people. You don't have to be like-minded, but you do have to learn the art of delegation. To me, it's trusting individuals either alongside you or underneath you... to make good corporate decisions which are ultimately aligned, with you behind them."

Sam, the CIO of a large financial services firm, was also clear about the value of reassigning requests to someone else: "Someone asked me to be on a steering committee. I looked at it, and for sure, I'm a great candidate to be on the steering committee, but I know I'm particularly oversubscribed at the moment. And I also have somebody that works in my group who, it would be good for her career development, so I passed on it and said, 'You should have this other person do it.'"

He went on to say, "There's another lens I put on it, too, and that's, 'Is this something I should be taking on myself or my team should be taking on?' So, it may have come to me and I could do it, and it is urgent, and it is really impactful, but am

I doing the organization a disservice by doing it myself, or is there an opportunity here for someone on my team? So [delegating] is something that makes its way into my head when I'm processing [requests]."

This statement is particularly powerful because he put as much emphasis on developing his team as he did on getting the request off his own plate (which is important for leaders in general). He also had the foresight to think about the organization and ensure the request and the developmental time were valuable to the organization. I appreciated Sam's mindset regarding the decision to delegate. He said, "I could do it," but all he's saying is that he has the ability to do it. That is certainly not a strong enough reason to say yes. However, he also said, "It is urgent." Remember that urgency alone does not make something a priority. In this case, however, Sam thought, "It is really impactful." This means the request aligned with his roadmap. It's impactful to him; it's impactful to the organization. If he couldn't, for whatever reason, delegate it to someone else, he would have a decision to make: Would something else on his plate need to be reprioritized?

Delegation is a powerful tool exercised by the most successful leaders and executives, and it can be used by anyone. The executives I spoke with used a delegation table to help them determine what types of requests to assign to which people. Their tables listed the team members, their skill sets, their interests, and their growth areas. Some junior managers believe it is easier to do everything themselves. However, when work is leveraged, much more can be accomplished. Delegation is a key skill set among this group, and perhaps another requirement for succeeding at this level.

The art of
delegation is one
of the key skills
any entrepreneur
must master.

RICHARD BRANSON

PRODUCTIVITY CORNER
Create a Delegation Table
_____

It's time to create your own delegation table. List all the people in your world to whom you could delegate projects or tasks. Then create a table that looks like this and fill in the fields:

PERSON	SKILLS	INTERESTS	GROWTH OPPORTUNITIES

When you receive a request that can be delegated because you are not the only one who can complete it, consult your table. If the request aligns with at least three out of the four items on the table, then bingo! Assign the request to that team member.

What if you want to delegate a request but there is no one to delegate it to? You'll need to create that perfect someone. I mean hire them, not birth them. You could try that too; it just may take a little longer. All those years of raking leaves as a kid—I'm convinced it was my father's strategy.

Five-Step Delegation Process

When you delegate a task to someone else, if you want to do it effectively, ask yourself the following questions and share your answers with the delegate:

1 **What does an outstanding result look like?**[1] Define a picture of it. If you have ever worked on a jigsaw puzzle, you know that it is nearly impossible to put the puzzle together

without the picture on the box. This is how clear your picture needs to be. When I onboarded a new administrative assistant, this is how I defined an outstanding result:

- All projects and tasks are tracked and updated.

- I am aware of a project status before asking.

- I am copied on all appropriate team and client communication.

- Meetings are attended on time.

- The assistant knows my schedule as well as I do.

- Priorities are always clear.

- When something cannot be done, commitments are renegotiated.

- The assistant anticipates my needs.

- The assistant follows scheduling protocol.

It's difficult to read a list like this and not know how to be successful. It is similar to giving the questions on the test before the day of the test. It positions people for success.

2 **Why is this task or job important?** Reasons are what drive our behavior and keep us on track. If the reasons are not strong enough, we will not get re-centered when we do fall off track. After I describe what an outstanding job looks like, I explain the reasoning behind the task. For example, an outstanding result accomplished by my administrative assistant enables me to work on business (writing, speaking, coaching). The outstanding result also makes the company look better. Finally, an outstanding result will help my administrative assistant in her career.

3   **How will you support this person to be successful?** Are
the team member's priorities clear? Will they have enough
time to complete this request? What support do they need
from others to be successful? Do they need any additional
training or mentoring?

In my example, I told the administrative assistant that
I would be responsive to requests, I would provide more
clarification when needed, and I would always support
her decisions when she had thought through the rationale,
even if I disagreed with the decision.

I encourage my team members to ask questions on items
that I have delegated because I have found that getting it
right the first time is less time-consuming than doing it
over again. It's always appropriate to ask the person, "What
support do you need from me on this?" Support may also
come from someone else.

4   **How would the person like to be held accountable?** I
love this coaching question because it empowers the person to decide. They may say, "I'll give you an update once
per week," or "I'll let you know when I need help," or "Could
we have a regular status meeting?"

My assistant and I use an online tool to track priorities
and progress. And we meet one-on-one two times a week to
review the status of projects, answer questions, and remove
roadblocks. When you ask this question and have a clear
answer, you will avoid the dreaded micromanagement. No
one likes micromanaging. Managers don't want to do it,
and those being managed don't want it. What are we managing anyway—micros? Focus on the outstanding result
and expect the person owning the task to figure out the rest.

5   **What's in it for them?** Go back to your delegation table.
Does the request align with their skills, interests, and growth

opportunities? In his book *Drive*, Dan Pink tells us that what motivates knowledge workers is mastery, autonomy, and purpose. Give people the chance to master a new skill, give them the autonomy to run with it, and discuss the underlying reason for the work. Help them ensure that the work is consistent with their own roadmap.

I recently had one of the coaches on my team ask to undertake some administrative work. At the time, she was still building her book of business, so she had time. My first question to her was, "What is your *reason* for wanting to take on this work?" She told me that it would keep her more connected to the organization, to me as the leader, and to other leaders. Then I told her I had mixed feelings about the approach. I had no doubt that she would be able to complete the work, excel at it, and bring it to levels that I was not thinking about. My only hesitation at the time was the question of whether it was best for her. Would it move her closer to building her coaching book of business? So, I asked her to contact someone else who was doing both administrative work and coaching. I said, "Let's learn from her and then discuss this again." After she spoke with the other person, she was more excited than ever. As we dug deeper, I learned that doing administrative work actually did align with her broader roadmap, and she could see that more clearly than I. It gave her the ability to do more work from home and reduced her commute, which gave her more time to focus on other goals like growing her business. It gave her the opportunity to learn more about our business, how we coach, and how we add value to clients. Within six months, she was loving the work, and I gave her a raise. She was providing the best work in that role and adding value in other ways.

So, think win-win. When you delegate, it's a win for you (you get something off your plate), and it's a win for them (they get to learn, grow, foster existing relationships, and build new relationships). When you have a conversation like this, the result may be that delegating the task to that person is not the best approach. This is still a victory because you have both learned something in the process.

In *It's a Wonderful Life*, we learn about the importance of developing others from George Bailey's father, Peter. Father and son are sitting together at the dining room table when Peter asks his son to consider taking over the Building and Loan.

> *Peter:* Of course, it's just a hope, but you wouldn't consider coming back to the Building and Loan, would you?... I know it's soon to talk about it.
>
> *George:* Oh, now, Pop, I couldn't. I couldn't face being cooped up for the rest of my life in a shabby little office. *He stops, realizing that he has hurt his father.*
>
> Oh, I'm sorry, Pop. I didn't mean that, but this business of nickels and dimes and spending all your life trying to figure out how to save three cents on a length of pipe... I'd go crazy. I want to do something big and something important.
>
> *Peter:* You know, George, I feel that in a small way we are doing something important. Satisfying a fundamental urge. It's deep in the race for a man to want his own roof and walls and fireplace, and we're helping him get those things in our shabby little office.

Here, Peter teaches George that great leaders help others get what they want in life. He teaches him how to help others take on more responsibility. He also teaches him the importance of compelling reasons.

KEY PRODUCTIVITY POINTS

- The most productive people consider delegating as an alternative to getting work done *and* as a development opportunity for the person taking on the assignment.

- Use a delegation table to identify the right person to assign a priority project to.

- Follow the Five-Step Delegation Process

  1. What does an outstanding result look like?
  2. Why is this task or job important?
  3. How will you support this person to be successful?
  4. How would this person like to be held accountable?
  5. What's in it for them?

PART THREE

Put It All to Work

Strategy is important, but execution is everything.

JEFF HADEN

8

Put the
Five Steps
into Action

1
Create your
roadmap

2
Define your
relationship hierarchy

3
Assess the quality
of the request

4
Prioritize and
reprioritize

5
Master
delegation

N OW THAT you know the Five Steps, let's put them to work.

When I think about learning a new skill, it always seems daunting at first. But over time and with practice, it becomes instinctive, and knowing when to say yes will too. When I transitioned from the corporate world to a coaching and training career, I knew very little about sales. It was a struggle, and I believed that I would never be good at it. I had a closing rate of 5 percent when I started. That means one person signed up out of every twenty. It was not enjoyable, and I almost gave up, but I knew I had to learn. I read a couple of books, hired a sales coach, and modeled the best people. As I watched, I thought about each step. I was conscious about it, I referred to notes, and eventually I got it: find out what's important to the client. Now it's second nature, I have a much higher closing rate, and I don't need to think about asking, "What's most important to the potential client?"

Another way to think of it is like this. Remember when you learned how to swing a golf club or a baseball bat and the instructor broke it down into steps for you, starting with, "Make sure your feet are in the right position"? In the case of golf, they then tell you to put the ball forward in your stance, to keep your front arm straight, to keep your head down, to bend your knees slightly, to backswing parallel to the ground, and to swing through the ball. If you needed to think about each of those steps every time, you'd never hit the ball! When you have muscle memory, it's almost automatic. How long did it take you to build that muscle memory?

The same goes for learning when to say yes. We want it to be intuitive, and it will not be automatic immediately. It will take repetition. Commit to the process, keep the cinnamon twist recipe the same, and it will all come together.

Five Weeks Is All It Takes

Now that you have the foundation to know when to say yes, you will be able to implement it in real time with ease. At this point your roadmap should be in place and documented, you have determined your relationship hierarchy, you know the five components of a quality request, and you are crystal clear about your priorities and know how to reprioritize when necessary. Just as you wouldn't decide to train for a 5K by setting out on a 5K run on the first day, I suggest an incremental five-week program.

Week 1, Step 1: Roadmap Test. For every request you get, simply focus on whether it is consistent with your roadmap (Productivity Corner, page 62). If it is, say yes; if it isn't, say no. And reward yourself each time you do this. Management experts often communicate, "What gets measured gets improved, and you can't manage it if you can't measure it." So, keep score. Track the number of requests you get during the week, the number that you accept, the number that you refuse, and when you use your roadmap to make the decision. You'll learn a great deal about the volume of requests that actually are consistent with your roadmap from simply doing this.

Week 2, Step 2: Relationship Test. For every request you get, focus on the requester and use your relationship hierarchy (Productivity Corner, page 92) to decide if you will say yes.

Week 3, Step 3: Truman Test. For every request you get, evaluate the quality of the request. Make sure it is respectful of your time, it is necessary, it is well thought out, it is clear and concise, and it has solutions. If it meets all five components, you're good to say yes. If not, ask the requester to fill in the gaps (Productivity Corner, page 106).

Week 4, Step 4: Reprioritize Test. For every request you get, focus on prioritizing. Nothing goes on your plate unless you understand its priority relative to everything else. Using your priority list (Productivity Corner, page 120), apply the priority test I describe in Chapter Six. Based on the size, will this fit into your roadmap? Will the timing required align with your other priorities? How urgent is the request? Is it a production outage, audit request, or something similar that will trump other priorities? Is it a prior commitment you want to honor? Is it a request from a client?

Use the Eisenhower matrix and ask yourself these questions: Is it urgent? Is it important? If it is a priority, accept the request. If it is not a priority—and I encourage a good use of this filter—then refuse the request. Track the yeses and nos and total them up.

Week 5, Step 5: Delegate and Pull It All Together. In the final week of the initial implementation, continue to use your delegation table (Productivity Corner, page 137) to identify if and to whom you can delegate requests.

In this final week, work toward integrating all Five Steps to Protect Your Time, and watch how your life changes!

1
Does it align with
my roadmap?

2
Who is
asking?

3
Is it a quality
request?

4
Where does it fit on
my priority list?

5
To whom can
I delegate?

Over these five weeks, you may find that you'll change your behavior simply through tracking. When I was losing weight in 2013, I tracked everything I ate. It went on a spreadsheet with total calories, fat grams, carbohydrate grams, and protein grams. That's all I tracked. I would sometimes make a decision on what I was going to eat based on what I wanted to record on the spreadsheet. How would it look to my trainer if I ate chocolate three times per day? There is a term for this in physics. What I mean is there is a term for the effect that measuring can have on a behavior, not for eating chocolate, although there probably should be a term for that too! It's called the observer effect, which simply means what you are measuring changes by the act of measuring. Pretty cool, huh?

Three Examples of the Five Steps in Practice

Allow me to share three examples of requests for my time, and how I used the Five Steps to Protect Your Time to decide.

Request Number 1

I received a voicemail message from a member of the corporate management team of a coaching organization I belong to. The request was to emcee a four-hour training event with five speakers and over five hundred attendees, two weeks away.

Did it align with my roadmap? Yes, the organization was important to me, and I wanted to contribute. Speaking is on my roadmap as well. I have a goal to secure more speaking engagements and be a better speaker. I love speaking because it is a chance to engage, entertain, and inspire others ✓ **YES**

Who was asking? The organization and the requester were high on my relationship hierarchy. I knew that the specific person making the request was speaking on behalf of the senior leadership of the organization. ✓ **YES**

Was it a quality request? The request was respectful of my time because it acknowledged the time commitment involved in accepting the request. It was necessary because having an emcee would free up the speakers to focus on their message. I felt like there was some missing information I needed to make a decision, which I got in a follow-up phone conversation. The request was also clear and concise. It met most but not all of the quality request components. ◐ **PARTIAL YES**

Where did the request fit on my priority list? First, I assessed how much time it would take me to prepare and deliver on the request. The time of the training event was open on my calendar, and I blocked time on my calendar to write and prepare my introductions and transitions. It was not a drop-everything-else request like a production outage or urgent client request would be, but I knew it would serve the community, help me sharpen my skills, and perhaps lead to other opportunities. ✓ **YES**

Could this project be delegated? Yes and no. It was not a request that I could delegate directly. If it had not met the other four steps, then I could have suggested other names that could fill the role. It came down to a yes or no, and I took twenty-four hours before making a final decision. What I could delegate was part of the preparation work. After developing a first draft of the script, I hired someone to review and edit it for me so it would be even better. ◐ **PARTIAL YES**

The final answer was a yes.

Request Number 2

I mentioned in Chapter One that I considered starting a podcast. There are many reasons to start a podcast: to share your ideas, to build a following, and to build credibility. They're more personal than a blog, and it would be fun to interact with smart, entertaining people. I thought this could support other goals on my roadmap.

Did it align with my roadmap? The key question was, should I add it to my roadmap? If I added it to my roadmap, it would support my coaching career, speaking career, and book sales. ✓ YES

Who was asking? Well, I was asking, and I am on my relationship hierarchy. I listen to requests from myself. As I like to say, it is okay to talk to yourself; it's even okay to answer. It's when you say "Huh?" that you have to worry. ✓ YES

Was it a quality request? I considered the time it would take to implement. I was not certain the podcast was necessary to grow my coaching, speaking, and book businesses. The request was certainly clear and concise, and included options on how to approach the podcast. ✓ YES

Where did the request fit on my priority list? Size and time were big factors on this decision. Some of it was unknown, and I would need to learn more before making a final decision. I did know that it required prep time, hiring someone to produce and edit the podcast, and blocking appropriate time on the calendar to record the episodes. ✗ NO

Could this project be delegated? I could hire someone to produce and edit the podcast. I didn't see a way to delegate the delivery and recording of the podcast. ◑ PARTIAL YES

The final answer was a no because too many other important items on the roadmap would need to be reprioritized to accommodate this wonderful idea of mine.

Request Number 3

I received a request to chair a committee in another coaching organization. The request came like this: "Lois resigned and can't take on the task. Nate doesn't want to do it. Gabrielle can't do it because she has other things going on. We really need someone. Would you be willing to do it?"

To answer this question, I put the Five Steps to work.

Did it align with my roadmap? Yes, the organization was important to me, and I wanted to contribute in some way. I also love a challenge and saw an opportunity to make things better. ✓ YES

Who was asking? The organization was not high on my relationship hierarchy. That didn't make the requester unimportant; it just meant that there were others that would be higher on the list. ✗ NO

Was it a quality request? The clarity of the request was there, although I did need to fill in a lot of details before I could make a final decision. I knew the requester didn't want it to sound this way, but it sounded like, "No one else wants to do it, so we're asking you." Believe me, I know this person, and he is a good, honest person. His intent was to get some help and get this important task done, but he hadn't completely thought through how to motivate me to want to accept the request. ✗ NO

Where did the request fit on my priority list? What would have to change for me to take on a fifty-hour project in eight weeks? That's over six hours per week, almost an hour a day. Something would have to be reprioritized. As I reviewed my other commitments, I was not able to free up that amount of time. ✕ **NO**

Could this project be delegated? The first answer is that it's irrelevant in this case since I decided to decline the request. The second answer is yes, it absolutely could be. I certainly could have done the work, and I would have done it well. I was not, however, the only person who could do it. I did brainstorm with the requester about other people who could fulfill the work that needed to be done, and we came up with a couple of great options. This is another way to delegate. It is not necessarily someone who works *for* you. We can get help in other ways. ◑ **PARTIAL YES**

I had to respectfully say no. And it was still a thoughtful and difficult decision for me. The roadmap almost overrode the other factors. That's the reason it is important to look at all the factors before making a decision.

Hopefully, you can now see how all Five Steps to Protect Your Time come together. To make sense of this, we need a matrix that looks like this:

REQUESTER	PRIORITY*	QUALITY	ROADMAP	DELEGATE	RESPONSE**
1	6	Y	Y	N	Y
2	4	N	N	N	N
Etc.					

* Priority number where it will fit on your list.
** Yes/No/Later

PRODUCTIVITY CORNER
Prepare Yourself for the New, Productive You

To get ready for your five-week journey, I invite you to take these three simple steps:

1   Review a request for your time that you have received in the last week, and apply the Five Steps. How did you initially respond? How does your response change after implementing the Five Steps?

2   Review a request you've made yourself and apply the Five Steps. What would you change, now that you know the Five Steps? How do the Five Steps help you prepare to make a request?

3   Identify an activity that you think is unproductive. Write it down. Now read the remainder of the chapter and then consider whether you still think it's unproductive.

What to Do When Your Instinct Still Says Yes

What happens when the five-step process tells you no and your instinct still says yes? Say yes if you review these five factors and it still feels right to you. Some of the most important work I've done is because I took a leap of faith and said yes. The purpose of this practice is to bring awareness to your yeses. It's not absolute. It's not scientific (well, the process was developed using science). At times, the Five Steps will tell you to say *no*, and you will still deep down want to say yes. Trust your intuition; there is something to that. At the same time, watch your frequency. If you find that you are still saying yes too much, then evaluate again and go back to the basics of the Five Steps.

When we are not productive, we're either working on the wrong things or paralyzed because we're not sure what we should be doing.

Be Productive Even When You're Not

Some will argue that they do not want to be productive every minute of every day. That's fine, and part of the rationale for this book was to help people break free from the busy trap. Ask yourself, what does not being productive look like to you? Maybe it's sitting and doing nothing, watching the sunset, having a cup of coffee with your favorite person in the world, or enjoying a dinner with friends. Maybe not being productive means you're golfing or cooking or playing a video game.

In a sense, though, when we do those things, aren't we still being productive? If we are sitting and doing nothing or watching the sunset, we are being mindful. We are in the moment, enjoying life. If we are having a cup of coffee with our favorite person, we are building a relationship, perhaps working on our relationship goals. We are saying yes to ourselves and the ones we love most.

When we are not productive, we're either working on the wrong things or paralyzed because we're not sure what we should be doing. It means that we're working on the right things but not as efficiently as possible.

So, when we implement the Five Steps to Protect Your Time, we are always productive. We are productive when we are working on our highest business goals. We are productive when we are being mindful. We are productive when we are spending time with a loved one.

KEY PRODUCTIVITY POINTS

- Five weeks is all it takes to make the Five Steps second nature. Focus and apply one of them each week for five weeks, and you will master them.

- These steps do not completely replace your intuition or common sense. Your intuition will become even stronger as you follow the Five Steps.

- Know that sometimes we feel we are not being productive, and yet what we are doing aligns with all the steps to protect our time.

Email is a system that delivers other people's priorities to your attention. It's up to you to decide when that priority should be managed into your world. It's not the other way around.

CHRIS BROGAN

9

Don't Check Email, Process It

SINCE YOU'VE STARTED using the Five Steps to Protect Your Time, you've likely noticed that every email you receive is a request for your time. Every one. This is true for messaging applications and for project collaboration tools.

In the early 1990s, when email was becoming ubiquitous, I was leading a committee that included a senior member of the community named Dave, who provided a service to technology customers. At the end of the committee meeting, I asked the group if it was okay for me to send the notes via email. I went around the group and captured everyone's email address, but when I got to Dave, he said, "I don't do email. I love the fax. One button, easy, and quick. Could you fax the notes to me?"

"Sure, Dave. What's your fax number?"

He thought for a couple of seconds, looked up as if he were searching deep in his brain for the number, and then replied, "I'm not sure. I will *email* it to you."

In the past three decades, email has become not only ubiquitous but, for many, overwhelming. Some people receive two hundred to three hundred messages per day and struggle to keep up.

One of my clients, whom I will call Tom, is an executive at a technology start-up. When we started working together, he had 15,474 email messages in his inbox and a reputation for not being responsive. He is a thought leader in his industry and well respected both inside and outside his company. He was often invited to speak at industry events to share his wisdom. All of these great strengths were in danger of being overshadowed by his lack of responsiveness to email, a common failing in today's fast-paced business world.

If we think of emails as requests for our time, we've taken the first step to conquering them, and we do that not by checking them but by processing them using the Five Steps to Protect Your Time. When I shared the title of this chapter with members of a community I belong to, the leader said, "Don, please don't pass out when I say this, but there were over twenty-five thousand messages in my inbox when you mentioned your chapter, and I now have it under five thousand!" And that was before she read this chapter. She accomplished that with the title only and without any of the strategies I'll provide in this chapter. I'm excited about the possibilities for you when you get control of your inbox. There's a feeling of lightness and freedom that comes with keeping your inbox to zero. You are not wondering what is lurking out there in the deep bowels of your inbox; you are not fearful that there is something you missed that could be career-limiting or life-changing.

Change the Language of Email

As I was writing this chapter, I was coming off three months of life-changing events. These events took much of my focus and created some amazing opportunities, and they forced me to change the way I work and interact. As a result, my email inbox was not as clean as I strive to keep it. Think about going from one dish and fork in the sink to overflowing dishes, pots, and pans in the sink and on the counter and unpleasant smells starting to arise.

I realized that I was *checking* email, and we need to stop doing that. The dictionary definition of "check" is "to inspect, examine, or look at appreciatively." Think about it: When we check email, we open a new message in the inbox, read it, and think, *Oh, that's a nice message; I appreciate it.* Then we close it and plan to deal with it later. Then we open the next one and think, *This request is too difficult to either respond to, delete, or file immediately, so I'll close it and move on to the next one.* We open the next one, and it's a message from a cool website company wanting us to sign up for a service or read their latest ideas. Close and move on to the next one.

Keep doing that with one hundred to three hundred email messages per day and you'll have thousands of messages in your inbox before you can blink. When you have a cluttered inbox, it clutters your mind. You scroll through messages you've read before, you miss messages that may require important action, and you find yourself constantly putting out fires. You had planned to address it, you had planned to respond and be prompt, but other things emerged and it got lost.

So, how do we stay on top of this continuous stream of messages, analogous to a leaky faucet that won't stop? Well, first stop "checking" email. When we check something, we are not taking action. What we need to do is approach email with an action-oriented, decision-making mindset. Remember that the words we use are the labels we put on our experiences. So let's use a more active, decisive word for checking email. Let's "process" it. When we process something, we take a series of actions for the purpose of some result. That's what we want. We want to take action on email, but that doesn't sound very elegant. "Process email" sounds much better.

What would happen if everyone stopped checking email? People would be more present. We would respond to email more quickly because we would be making decisions and taking appropriate action. We would be more productive without that constant need to peek and see who needs something from us now. We get a dopamine hit each time we see that bold message sitting at the top of our inbox or spot that notification popping up at the bottom of our screen or hear that notification sound. We love dopamine because it feels good, and that short-term hit is the reason we love to "check" email. However, the long-term impact of that short-term boost is a heaviness, the feeling of being overwhelmed that comes with potentially thousands of emails sitting in our inbox. According to an article published in the *Daily Mail,* 92 percent of employees become stressed when they receive and read an email message, leading to higher blood pressure and heart rates.[1]

Will you help me change the vernacular? Tell everyone that you're *processing* your email.

Take Back Control

The first step is to sort your inbox by date and time received in *ascending* order. That means the oldest one first. First in, first out; it's only fair. For years, I processed the most recent emails first, until it occurred to me that the older ones might never get processed. When you process the oldest emails first, you get the reward of processing the newer ones at the end. And it is a reward.

When you open an email, you must make a decision about it using the Five Steps, because it is a request for your time. Will you accept the request, decline the request, or delegate it? If you accept the request, will you do it now or later? Your options as you process the email are as follows:

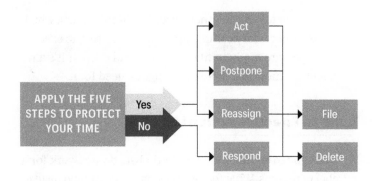

1 **Act.** If it's a yes, take action on it now and then file or delete the email.

2 **Postpone.** If you are going to postpone for future action, you must capture it in your action system, which we'll discuss next. Your inbox is *not* your action system. Once you have captured that, you can file it in a folder for reference.

3 **Reassign.** You may choose to forward this message to a colleague for more information or for completion. Same as step two, please file it for reference and track the follow-up in your action system; note that you are waiting for this to be completed by the person to whom you delegated. Waiting for something is a type of action, and we want to track those actions.

4 **Respond.** Respond to the requester, explain your decision, and either delete or file the email.

5 **File or delete.** At some point, either immediately or after you take action, you must move it out of your inbox. Move it to a folder for future reference. I suggest creating subfolders in your mailbox for categories. For example, categories may include Team, Clients, Finance, Family, Friends, Admin. Your email tool will likely sort those from A to Z. Keep only

one level of folders. In other words, avoid subfolders, which create unnecessary complexity. This is very easy to execute when you are ready to file. You drag and drop. If it's a no, delete the message; there's no longer a need for it.

Build an Effective Action List

As I mentioned in Chapter One, to-do lists do not work for a number of reasons. What follows are what I recommend instead.

1 **Track your actions in a list or system that you'll actually use.** This can be an electronic system or a paper system, whichever you prefer. I happen to prefer an electronic system because it is available on my laptop and my smartphone, or any device with internet connection, for that matter. For my current preferred list of tracking tools, please go to my website WhentoSayYes.com.

2 **When you put an item on the list, make it actionable.** In other words, don't put "book" on your action list, put an action verb in front of it. For example, are you planning to buy a book, read a book, or start writing a book? As I mentioned in Chapter One, be as specific as possible.

3 **Keep the list absolutely, 100 percent prioritized.** See Chapter Six to help you.

4 **Organize the list based on where it will get done.** When you need your computer to do something like send emails, research a topic, or write an article, put that on a list called Computer. If you need to call your dealer (I'm thinking car dealer; what were you thinking?) or insurance company or mom, put all of that on a list labeled Calls. For someone you meet with regularly, create a list just for that person.

I meet with my coaching team biweekly, and every time something presents itself that would be a useful conversation for our one-on-one meeting, it goes on my list for that person. If it can't wait, then email or text.

5   **Keep a separate Waiting list.** This useful tip comes from David Allen's Getting Things Done system. A Waiting list is great for projects or tasks that you have delegated, and it's important for you to know when they're complete. Put the delegated item on this list, date it, and follow up at appropriate times. You will never lose track of something you are waiting for again with this list—it's a life-changer.

Processing Email on Smart Devices

It's also acceptable to process email on your smart device. Please note that I said "process," not "check." If you want to process email on your smart device, a few things need to be set up. If you don't take these steps, you risk reading them twice (and think about how inefficient that is), or worse, losing track of them. First, the device must synchronize with your desktop. This means that when you delete an email or file an email to a folder on your device, these changes also occur on your desktop or laptop. If you're not sure how to set this up, search and find a solution online. When you do this, you will have the same actions available on your phone as on your desktop or laptop.

Next, review the options on your email app so that it is easy to delete and file emails. I have set up my email app (I use Outlook) so that if I swipe right, the app offers me folders to file the message. If I swipe left, it deletes the message. These are the two most common actions for me. Take a look at the options

No one ever got rich checking their email more often.

NOAH KAGAN

your email program offers you. I also have a way to capture an action on my action list right from the email app if required.

Once you have this all set up, you can use the Five Steps to process email on your smartphone and be assured that you will do it effectively and efficiently. One caveat is that I am not suggesting processing email while you are in a meeting or with other people. If you do that, you are back to multitasking, and we know the dangers and downfalls of that.

How to Catch Up

Have you ever heard the riddle, "How do you eat an elephant?" The answer is, "One bite at a time." When it comes to catching up on email after a vacation or being ill, or simply after weeks, months, or years of neglect, we need to chunk the problem into bites. I have seen clients and students with anywhere from thirty to ninety-nine thousand messages in their inbox. If you have more than one hundred messages in your inbox, then you need a catch-up strategy.

Take the following steps:

Tackle the most recent emails first. Create a folder named @Process. The @ sign will force it to sort to the top. Move anything older than two weeks into it. Process the messages that remain in your inbox using the method described above. Continue until there are zero messages in your inbox.

Tackle the older messages in the @Process folder. Do this in thirty-minute chunks. Keep track of how many emails you can process in that window so you will know how to block your time for processing email moving forward. If you can process one hundred messages in thirty minutes, and you have three thousand messages in your inbox, you'll be completely caught up in a month. The more messages you have, the more likely they'll be dated, and the more likely you'll be able to process even more in thirty minutes.

If you want to overachieve and get there faster, I'm right there with you: go for it. The following strategies will help you work with maximum efficiency within each thirty-minute session.

- **Sort by subject first.** The reason this is useful for a large number of messages is that you can usually read the last one and file them all together. For example, my coaching team had an email exchange about leadership. The subject was "leadership definition." Several people replied and commented, all building on the previous message. If I were processing email after an absence and I sorted by subject, I would see all of those messages together. Then I could read the last one only, and delete or file the others.

- **Next, sort by sender.** You may be able to delete or file many messages together when you take this approach. For example, I get quote alerts from my online brokerage company every thirty minutes. When I sort by sender, I can easily see all of those together, highlight them, and delete. It feels good writing it, and even better when you actually do it.

- **Use the Unsubscribe button liberally.** If there are messages from certain senders sitting unread in your inbox, there's a good chance that you'll never want to see these messages again, so unsubscribe. If you continue to receive messages from a sender after you have unsubscribed, most email systems allow you to set up a rule. A rule would look like this: "If message received from sender ABC Company, move message to Deleted Items folder."

PRODUCTIVITY CORNER
Empty Your Inbox

Your action plan for this chapter is to get to zero in your inbox by the end of today. Not tomorrow, not next week, not next month. Do it today. Move anything older than two weeks into a folder for later, and process the rest. The only messages that will be left in your inbox at this point are those from the past two weeks. Good luck! I'm right there with you, looking over your shoulder, helping you make good decisions about each email.

Once you're done, take a moment to congratulate yourself! You are one step closer to being current on email. You know exactly what you need to do and exactly what you don't need to do. Email monsters that used to lurk in your inbox waiting to attack or explode at the worst possible time no longer exist or are less scary. You killed the monsters. That feeling of guilt, wondering if you responded to every request you need to respond to, has disappeared. You are not apprehensive about finding that urgent email every three minutes because you are confident you will get to it at the right time, and in enough time. You're on top of email instead of at the bottom. You are in control of your email; it is not controlling you. I imagine that you feel freer and less weighed down without hundreds or thousands of emails.

How to Stay Current

Now that you have all the skills and discipline you need to process your mail, here are the steps you can take to stay on top of it. I suggest starting with processing your email only three times per day—for example, at eight a.m., twelve p.m., and five p.m. Adjust these times to meet your schedule. The idea is that you process only three times per day—beginning, middle, and end. Outside of those times, don't "check" email because that will bring you down the rabbit hole of opening and closing emails and not taking action. When you do the often-termed "urgent scan" of email, you may not be taking action, and that's how your email accumulates and your inbox gets clogged. Think about it: if someone absolutely needs you before your next check (about four hours), then they will find a way to get you, usually by phone or text. Or *you* could create an urgent way for your top requesters to get you if you they need you during focused time.

Let's assume you get 150 emails per day. I realize that some of you will be getting more than that and some will be getting fewer. This is a guideline. Let's also assume that they are evenly distributed throughout the day. You'll have roughly fifty emails in your inbox at each process point in the day. I almost wrote *check*point there, but that would defeat the whole point of this chapter, *because we are not checking email anymore.* How long will it take you to process fifty emails? If you can process each one in thirty to sixty seconds, you're going to be fine with a thirty-minute session. You may or may not need to block time for this in your calendar. If you find that you're constantly behind on your email, consider blocking more time on your calendar to process.

Once you've experimented a bit, you may find you need to add one or two more processing times a day because your office culture demands a quicker than four-hour response time on emails. Before you jump to that, however, do an honest assessment: Is that actually the culture, or is that your interpretation of it?

There are things your company can do to ensure that everyone stays current on email. As I wrote this chapter, my team and I decided we needed to establish our email standards together. We were reviewing our team agreements, and one member said, "Respond to all emails within twenty-four hours." There was concern that we wouldn't all be able to live up to that. So, a couple of us got together, created a proposal, and then reviewed it with the group.

Here's what we decided:

1 **Include the subject, action required, and date it's required in the subject line.** We wanted to make it easy for those reading email messages to understand what we wanted them to do. So right in the subject line, in all caps, we include "FYI" if it is informational only, "Please respond by [date]" if feedback is requested, or "Action required by [date]" if the email includes a request for action.

2 **Respond within the agreed-upon time for internal and external messages.** We decided that for clients we would respond in twelve business hours. For everyone else (partners, team members, vendors), we would respond within one business day.

3 **Follow messaging etiquette.** We established the following rules:

- Use text if the request is urgent (same-day response).

- Senders can send a reminder email on Action emails.

- No response means agreement or no input to give.

- Use "reply all" sparingly.

- Use your judgment when replying all with one-liners (e.g., thanks, thank you, great, loved it).

- When forwarding an email, include your comments or intended outcome.

- If the topic of the conversation has changed, change the subject to stay current with the conversation at hand.

- Use the standard signature template for desktop email and on your phone app.

- For sensitive topics that have resulted in more than three email exchanges, pick up the phone.

- Proofread, spell check, and review the recipient list for every message.

- Use realistic timelines (not every email is urgent).

- Remember that nothing is confidential in email and email is permanent.

PRODUCTIVITY CORNER
Your Email Action Plan

If you have not already taken action on my recommendations in this chapter, I invite you now to execute the following action plan:

- Move all email messages more than two weeks old to a new @Process folder that you can come back to later to catch up on email.

- Sort your inbox by oldest email.

- Process all emails remaining in your inbox so you are completely up to date and there are no emails remaining in your inbox.

- Schedule time on your calendar to process the older emails. It does not have to be all in one sitting. In fact, I would recommend that you break it into several sessions, with short chunks of time for each.

KEY PRODUCTIVITY POINTS

- Every email you receive is a request for your time.

- Take back control of your email by shifting your mindset from checking email to processing email.

- Build an effective action list by transforming the items on your to-do list into actionable items, 100 percent prioritized, and organized by how the items will get done (e.g., calls, computer, or face-to-face).

Congratulations, by implementing the concepts in this chapter, you have arrived at the other side of email.

Better it is to live one day wise and meditative than to live a hundred years foolish and uncontrolled.

BUDDHA

Be Your Most Productive Self

YOU ARE AMAZING! You've made it this far, which means that you understand the basics for making great decisions about requests for your time. If you have followed along all the way, you have a roadmap and you know how to match requests against that. You have a ranked list of your most important requesters. Your ability to recognize a quality request versus one that is not ready for you has improved. You have a ranked list of priorities and have built the skills to reprioritize only when necessary. You are on your way to mastering delegation and knowing exactly to whom and when to delegate. And you've executed the Five Steps to take control of your email. Congratulations! You have the building blocks to take your productivity beyond what you may have imagined when you started this book.

In this chapter, I'm going to show you a few ways that you can integrate the Five Steps with other productivity tools.

Optimize Your Calendar

Time holds much value for me, and being on time for appointments is important. I would rather be an hour early than five minutes late. So, I think backwards. For example, if I need to be in Boston for a noon lunch meeting, I allow thirty minutes for travel time (middle of the day, and not likely to have traffic), fifteen minutes to park, necessary walking or Uber time, and another fifteen minutes of buffer time depending on the importance of the meeting. So, that may get me out of the house at 10:30. If you don't allow for transition and buffer time, you are going to be late. There's actually a word for this in Swedish, *tidsoptimist,* which literally means "time optimist" and refers to someone who is habitually late because they believe they have more time than they really do.

Could we apply this same concept to your daily calendar? When planning out your week, make sure you have blocked time for priorities you have committed to, and allow for buffer time and transition time. Avoid being completely booked so that you have slack for the unexpected.

The calendar is a noteworthy tool that the most productive people use to manage requests for their time. When I surveyed business leaders, all but one agreed with the comment, "I carry a calendar with me to record appointments," and two-thirds said they always carried it with them. Sam, who has a big job as a CIO leading 2,500 IT people, said he boiled his management down to two things: a notebook and a calendar. "The process I use is, I've got my list—my notebook with my list of items to process—and I've got my calendar, which is the sum total of all my prior commitments."

Here's the idea. We trust our calendar more than any other productivity tool. Think about it. You put stuff on your to-do list and then never read it again. Okay, maybe you don't do this all the time. Conversely, when you put appointments and meetings on your calendar, you always trust yourself to look there. You are not thinking about what you have to do at eleven a.m. next Wednesday because you know your calendar will remind you where you need to be.

So rather than simply using your calendar to track meetings and appointments, how about using it as a reminder of important goals and projects? This concept is known as time-blocking—we decide how much time a project will take and then block it on the calendar. Here's the way it works. Say, for instance, you get an email requesting your time on a project. You process the email, apply the Five Steps, and decide you'll take it on. The next thing you'll do is add that project to your priority list and your calendar.

For example, when I decided I wanted to write this book, I determined where it fell in my priority list. I then did a bit of research and learned that I needed to write about forty thousand words. Next, I set a target date of when I wanted it completed, and then I worked backward. I set a target to write one hour each day. Then, I counted the number of writing days I had between the start and end dates. I didn't write most weekends (although, funny—I'm writing this section on a Saturday), and I skipped days when I was delivering client training (usually two days at a time) because the days were already blocked for that activity and clients are high on my relationship hierarchy. I counted 109 days. On those days, I set up a recurring appointment with myself for one hour to write. In that hour, I did nothing else: no email, no text messages, no phone calls, no browsing cat videos, no searching for the best restaurants. Writing, and only writing.

To help you schedule your time, consider the rock metaphor, original source unknown, although I first learned it from Stephen Covey in *The Seven Habits of Highly Effective People*. A philosophy professor starts his class with a jar on the desk. Without speaking, he takes big rocks and puts them in the jar all the way to the top. Then he asks the class, "Is the jar full?"

The class confirms that the jar is full.

Work expands
to fill the
time allotted.

PARKINSON'S LAW

Then, the professor takes pebbles, and pours the pebbles into the jar all the way to the top. Again, he asks the class, "Is the jar full?"

The class confirms that the jar is full.

Then, the professor takes a bucket of sand and pours it into the jar, all the way to the top. And again, he asks the class, "Is the jar full?"

And once again, the class confirms that the jar is full.

Then, he takes a bucket of water, and the sand absorbs all the water.

The point here is that you cannot get the big rocks in the jar if you put the water or sand in first. In my coaching work with dental teams, I teach dentists how to use this concept in their business. If you're a dentist running a $1 million practice, your time is worth $685 dollars per hour. So dentists need to make the most efficient use of their time. In our "schedule to goal" program, we ask them to set a goal, because you can't schedule to goal unless you *have* a goal. The next thing they do is block time, usually two to three hours per day in two separate blocks, for their most productive procedures. They are not allowed to put any less-productive (pebbles or sand), and certainly non-productive (water), procedures in those slots.

So, what are your rocks? Pull out your priority list.

Priority 1 = Rocks
Priority 2 = Pebbles
Priority 3 = Sand
Priority 4 = Water

When you're blocking time in your calendar, block out the rocks first. For example, block time for yourself and your health, exercise, family, and vacations first. What do you need to work on every single day? Design your year, design your life.

If you are not designing it, then someone else is. Do you want to work on *your* goals or someone else's goals?

What are your pebbles?

What is your sand?

What is your water?

I know from many clients that it is easy to block the time on your calendar and more difficult to honor the calendar. This is where we come back to our compelling reasons, discussed in Chapter Three. Our compelling reasons will keep us focused on the important priorities that we have time-blocked, and from getting pulled into text, email, and browsing. So, write your compelling reasons right on your calendar. For example, "Hire IT Support Manager (so that I will regain eight hours per week)."

The other reason that we may get pulled into cat videos or something just as fruitless is that the work on goals is difficult. It's not easy to replace lost revenue, restructure the organization, write a performance improvement plan, or start a new business. It's much easier to reply to an email or watch a video than to make significant progress on your goals. To be productive, we must focus. As my coach, Gabriel, tells me, the first thing you have to do is "get in the right emotional state, and the second thing you have to do is *stay* in the right emotional state." In other words, decide what emotional state you need to be in when you are about to tackle that goal. Is it excited, inspired, empathetic, caring, intelligent, or creative? Decide which emotional state will serve you most on that goal, and put yourself there.

Work consistently and regularly, and you will make progress on your goals. Michael Jordan didn't become the best basketball player in the world in the nineties because of his talent. He became the best player in the world because he practiced consistently every day on his goals.

Process Meeting Invitations

We get meeting invitations all day long. How do you evaluate a meeting invitation? Here's what I suggest: the same way you would any other request for your time—based on your roadmap, the relationship, the priority, and the quality of the request. In this specific case, here are some items we can evaluate:

- Am I absolutely critical for the meeting?
- Is there an agenda?
- Is the outcome clear?
- Do I have time to prepare for the meeting?

Think about your calendar as the sum total of all of your prior commitments, including meetings. I advocate scheduling your most important goals and priorities on your calendar, but there's this phenomenon going on in corporate America right now where people's calendars are not their own. Anyone who wants to schedule a meeting can open a scheduling tool, determine when everyone has openings, and schedule the meeting. But here's the thing. This is still a request for your time. We all need to be conscious about these requests, process them through our system, and accept or reject (politely) based on the result. If you default to accept, you know what happens. Your schedule is full, there's no time to work on your goals, there's certainly no time to stay current on email, and you fall further and further behind.

You have two choices. On the one hand, you can avoid this when you block time on your calendar. To others, it will look like you are always busy, forcing a conversation and a real request for your time. In other words, let's not make it easy for people to steal our most precious asset—our time.

On the other hand, if you want to avoid having people calling or interrupting you, there may be a benefit to allowing others to schedule you into meetings, so long as your priorities and goals have already been scheduled. Luke, the tech CEO, was intentional about the way he used his calendar: "If I allow people to consume all my time, I know I will not be productive. So, I tend to try allocating some time in my calendar... Generally, I insist on people making a calendar entry. If somebody really wants my time and it could be a review of a document or whatever, they've got to send a calendar invite." Andrew, a partner in an information tech and business consulting firm, also prefers requesters ask for time on his calendar: "Sure, set up some time. Please look at my calendar [and] let me know what it is."

When considering a meeting request, also keep in mind Parkinson's Law, which states that the work expands to the time allotted. So, you may ask yourself if the time is appropriate to the work that needs to be done. Could the outcome of the meeting be accomplished in less time? In other words, you may want to accept the meeting but ask for less time. Have you ever attended a meeting that ended early? I'll bet you have, and I will also bet that most of your meetings run the full time allotted or longer. It does not have to be that way. Which ones feel better—the shorter ones or longer ones? I advocate that meetings can be more efficient and more effective, and it's almost always better to end early.

Mindfulness, Not Multitasking

The first time I tried yoga was several years ago at a mini-retreat in Western Massachusetts. My wife and I went together

I must govern the clock, not be governed by it.

GOLDA MEIR

and signed up for a yoga class. At the very beginning of the class, the instructor had us do a mindfulness exercise. She asked us to sit cross-legged with upright posture. She then led us through a brief guided exercise to be fully present. I observed the surroundings, glanced at my wife once or twice. Then she called us together. "What did you observe during this mindfulness time?" she asked. She was clearly looking for some amazing internal reflection about ourselves, perhaps some eureka moment.

I was thrilled to share what I observed. I said, "There are exactly 322 ceiling tiles." She was not thrilled with my snarky response.

Although my first jaunt with yoga and meditation was not successful, I have come to see the benefits of meditating specifically on focus and productivity. High-performing leaders use mindfulness as a productivity tool. Mindfulness is about being in the present moment and nowhere else. It is about quieting the mind of all distractions. Rasmus Hougaard and Jacqueline Carter define mindfulness as "enhancing focus and awareness both in work and in life." According to them, focus and awareness are the skills that define a mindful mind. "More explicitly, focus is the ability to concentrate on what you're doing in the moment, while awareness is the ability to recognize and release unnecessary distractions as they arise."[1] Matt Killingsworth's app, Track Your Happiness, reports that people using the app spend 47 percent of their time not focused on the task at hand. Mindfulness is the opposite of multitasking.

I acknowledge that focusing is difficult to do these days. It's challenging for us to stay in the present moment because there's a great deal vying for our attention. The good news is that practicing mindfulness improves cognitive function and increases productivity.[2]

A research study done at Massachusetts General Hospital correlated meditation with structural changes in the brain. The eight-week mindfulness meditation program led to an increase in gray-matter density in the part of the brain responsible for learning and memory (temporal lobe) and a decrease in the hippocampus, the area responsible for anxiety and stress responses.[3]

At General Mills, employees who attended only one program on mindfulness reported a significant increase in productivity:

- 83 percent of participants said they were taking time each day to optimize their personal productivity—up from 23 percent before the course.

- 82 percent said they were now making time to eliminate tasks with limited productivity value—up from 32 percent before the course.

- 80 percent of senior executives who took the course reported a positive change in their ability to make better decisions, while 89 percent said they became better listeners.[4]

The bottom line is that mindfulness *works* and makes us more productive. One-third of the participants in my study practiced some level of mindfulness, whether they called it that or not. Luke shared with me, "Because the whole concept of people asking for my time generally implies a disruption... I tend to try to focus in the evening following the day. I'll set aside maybe an additional hour or two hours or whatever." And James, the CIO of a midsize financial service firm, said, "I've got to have some quiet time. I don't want to start it when I'm constantly being interrupted, because then I just feel like I'm being reactive."

Mindfulness and your calendar are essential parts of your productivity tool kit. If you do not make the most of them, you'll continue to be busy rather than purposely productive.

And you didn't read this far in the book to be less productive. When you do maximize both tools, you will start to see your output increase and your productivity levels soar, and the effects of that will start to domino and affect other parts of your life.

As you enter the final chapter of this book, you are capable of accomplishing things now that may have seemed impossible or at least improbable before. You are set for amazing things. In a way, this is a brand-new beginning for great things ahead. Enjoy the process!

PRODUCTIVITY CORNER
Practice Mindfulness

To ease yourself into practicing mindfulness, start with five or ten minutes in the morning. Sitting upright, close your eyes and take several slow, deep breaths in through your nose and out through your mouth. If your mind wanders, that is totally fine; simply make a mental note and come back to breathing. I find it helpful to count my breaths—that keeps me focused on the breath versus other things that may have my attention.

Many tools help you with practicing mindfulness. Please go to WhentoSayYes.com to see my latest recommendations on the best mindfulness and meditation apps. Download them and make it a daily practice.

I invite you to take the following calendar actions as well:

- Set daily time aside to meditate and practice mindfulness.

- Review all of your recurring meetings and decide which ones will stay.

- Block time on your calendar for your most important goals.

KEY PRODUCTIVITY POINTS

- Your calendar is your most important productivity tool.

- Apply the Five Steps to all meeting invitations you receive.

- People who practice mindfulness are more productive.

Conclusion
Anything Is Possible!

LARRY BIRD is arguably one of the top ten basketball players of all time, and one of my favorites. Hey, I'm from Boston, and I grew up in the eighties when the Celtics won three championships and the rivalry between the Lakers and Celtics, between Magic and Bird, was at its peak. That rivalry, in some ways, catapulted the National Basketball Association into popularity. Bird is one of the most focused athletes I have watched. He started playing basketball at age thirteen to follow in his brother's footsteps, and he loved it. He knew he wanted to play professional basketball and worked at it. He's not the fastest guy on the court; in fact, he was somewhat clunky when it came to running up and down the court. However, his instincts of where the ball would be, how to make the perfect shot, and how to make the perfect pass were almost unrivaled.

Early in his career, his agent, Bob Woolf, asked him to do a television commercial. Bird felt this would take his focus away from playing basketball, so he refused. His agent asked him again, this time for a lot more money, and he refused. A few months later, his agent asked him again, still escalating the offers, and Larry said, "Mr. Woolf, all I want to do is play basketball."

It's pretty clear that, like many of the leaders I spoke to, consciously or subconsciously, Bird considered his roadmap, the requester, the quality of the request, and the priority of the request to reach that decision. Bird was über-successful in many ways, and these factors allowed him to maintain that focus. Later in his career, he did make some well-done, entertaining commercials, including one with Michael Jordan that was aired during a Super Bowl.

You now have the Five Steps to Protect Your Time and a productivity toolkit that will allow you to be your most productive self. You are crystal clear about what should be on your action list and what needs to go. You have a much shorter list of commitments than when you started. You now have a systematic way to evaluate new requests for your time in email, in meetings, in person, and in any other request medium, for that matter. You know exactly when to say yes—and when to say no.

George Bailey ultimately arrived at a similar place in *It's a Wonderful Life*. At the end of the movie, the lesson is that if you have friends, you are successful. George always listened to his own voice when he was confronted with those tough choices: follow his dreams or serve his community? He stuck around to run the business when his father died; he stuck around when his brother decided not to take over the family business. He refused Potter's job offer to travel and make significantly more money. He refused the job from his friend Sam Wainright so he could continue to serve his community. Although George didn't feel that successful, Clarence the angel helped him connect the dots among all of his successes, showing him how important he was to the culture of the community.

George sees what the world would be like without him. He sees Potter take over Bedford Falls, now called Pottersville. Pottersville is a different kind of town from Bedford Falls, lined with casinos and nightclubs. George's real estate development, Bailey Park, does not exist. He sees his favorite bar owned by someone other than his friend Martini, and it is a much less friendly place. Because George was not there to save him, his brother died as a young boy, never became a soldier, and, therefore, didn't save the US troops on a transport and become a war hero. His uncle Billy ends up in a mental institution, the pharmacist serves a twenty-year prison sentence for poisoning the boy, and Mary never marries. "Strange, isn't it?" asks Clarence. "Each man's life touches so many other lives. When he isn't around, he leaves an awful hole, doesn't he?"

And when George sees the differences between a world with him and a world without him, he is overjoyed with the former. I can see that smile on his face as he's holding his young daughter at the end of the movie. Although it seemed like he was not following his roadmap throughout these decisions—"I know what I am going to do tomorrow, and the next day, and the day after that. I'm shakin' the dust of this crummy little town off my feet..."—he actually was following what was important to him—his family, his community. He simply needed a bit of divine intervention to realize it. Perhaps this book is all the intervention you need.

What is your real roadmap?

I know that changing the world is possible for you too. George changed the world. We know what the world would have looked like without him. It would have been run by Mr. Potter, a world of gambling and alcohol and everyone crawling to a tyrant. Sometimes the world we want to change is the whole world, as Steve Jobs or Jeff Bezos did. Sometimes the world we want to change is our own small part of the world—our company, our community, our family and friends. You *will* make that world better because you are in it.

Changing the world may have seemed impossible when you started this book, because you were busy. You had too much on your plate, and you weren't serving any of your projects as effectively as possible. Now you have time to do what is on your plate more effectively and at a higher level. Now that you are purposely productive, you can create the world you want and excel.

You will make
the world
better because
you are in it.

Acknowledgments

THANK YOU TO...

Ghada, who gives me the space I need to be creative and the inspiration to be my best self.

AJ Harper and Top Three Workshop, for a clear writing process and, more importantly, a process for showing up and beating the trolls every day.

My Fielding cohort, the GTD Circle, who supported me throughout my research, and without whom there would have been no dissertation, no PhD, and no book.

My Fortune Management family, who continue to impress me and encourage me to imagine what's possible beyond my limitations.

My publisher, Page Two, who made this a far better book than it ever would have been.

You, the reader, for purchasing the book and reading it to the end. Here's to you being purposely productive.

Appendix

The Five Steps to Protect Your Time

1 Create your roadmap.
2 Define your relationship hierarchy.
3 Assess the quality of the request.
4 Prioritize and reprioritize.
5 Master delegation.

Five-Step Delegation Process

1 What does an outstanding result look like?
2 Why is this task or job important?
3 How will you support this person to be successful?
4 How would the person like to be held accountable?
5 What's in it for them?

Five Components of a Quality Request

1 It is respectful of your time.
2 It is necessary.
3 It is well thought out.
4 It is clear and concise.
5 It includes solutions.

Seven Factors to Determine Priority

1 Size
2 Time

3 Urgency
4 Prior Commitments
5 Audit and Regulatory Requests
6 Client Requests and Customer Satisfaction
7 Production Outages

Five Options When Processing Email

1 Act
2 Postpone
3 Reassign
4 Respond
5 File or delete

Five Steps to Create an Action List

1 Track your actions in a list or system that you'll actually use.
2 When you put an item on the list, make it actionable.
3 Keep the list absolutely, 100 percent prioritized.
4 Organize the list based on where it will get done.
5 Keep a separate waiting list.

Notes

Chapter 1: Break Out of the Busy Trap

1. Helen Kirwan-Taylor, "The Myth of Multi-tasking," *Management Today*, November 2009, 50–51.
2. Adapted from an exercise in Dave Crenshaw, *The Myth of Multi-tasking: How "Doing It All" Gets Nothing Done* (San Francisco: Jossey-Bass, 2008).
3. Kep Kee Loh and Ryota Kanai, "Higher Media Multi-tasking Activity Is Associated with Smaller Gray-Matter Density in the Anterior Cingulate Cortex," *PLOS ONE* 9, no. 9 (2014): e106698, https://doi.org/10.1371/journal.pone.0106698.
4. Stephen R. Covey, Foreword to *Prisoners of Our Thoughts: Viktor Frankl's Principles for Discovering Meaning in Life and Work,* by Alex Pattakos and Elaine Dundon (Oakland, CA: Berrett-Koehler, 2017), x.

Chapter 2: Be Purposely Productive

1. Sarah Rudell Beach, "10 Words to Use Instead of 'Busy,'" *HuffPost*, February 25, 2015, huffpost.com/entry/10-words-to-use-instead-o_b_6685794.
2. Shane Frederick, "Cognitive Reflection and Decision Making," *Journal of Economic Perspectives* 19, no. 4 (2005): 25–42, https://doi.org/10.1257/089533005775196732.
3. James G. March, "Theories of Choice and Making Decisions," *Society* 20, no. 1 (1982): 29–39, https://doi.org/10.1007/bf02694989.
4. Hal R. Arkes and Catherine Blumer, "The Psychology of Sunk Cost," *Organizational Behavior and Human Decision Processes* 35, no. 1 (1985): 124–40, https://doi.org/10.1016/0749-5978(85)90049-4.

5. Todd R. Zenger, "Why Do Employers Only Reward Extreme Performance? Examining the Relationships Among Performance, Pay, and Turnover," *Administrative Science Quarterly* 37, no. 2 (1992): 198–219, https://doi.org/10.2307/2393221.

6. Joyce Ehrlinger, Wilson O. Readinger, and Bora Kim, "Decision-Making and Cognitive Biases," *Encyclopedia of Mental Health*, ed. Howard S. Friedman, 2nd ed. (Oxford: Academic Press, 2016): 5–12, https://doi.org/10.1016/B978-0-12-397045-9.00206-8.

7. Susan T. Fiske and Shelley E. Taylor, *Social Cognition: From Brains to Culture* (London: Sage, 2013).

8. Ap Dijksterhuis, "Think Different: The Merits of Unconscious Thought in Preference Development and Decision Making," *Journal of Personality and Social Psychology* 87, no. 5 (2004): 586–98, https://doi.org/10.1037/0022-3514.87.5.586.

Chapter Four: Define Your Relationship Hierarchy

1. Terry Bacon, *What People Want: A Manager's Guide to Building Relationships that Work* (Mountain View, CA: Davies-Black, 2006).

2. Zig Ziglar, *Secrets of Closing the Sale* (Grand Rapids, MI: Revell, 2019), 37.

3. Bernie Stoltz, personal conversation with author.

Chapter Six: Prioritize and Reprioritize

1. Robert C. Pozen, *Extreme Productivity: Boost Your Results, Reduce Your Hours* (New York: HarperCollins, 2012).

2. Laverne Forest and Sheila Mulcahy, "First Things First: A Handbook of Priority Setting in Extension" (University of Wisconsin-Extension, Division of Program and Staff Development, 1976), 64.

3. Kevin Ashton, "Why (and How) Creative People Need to Say 'No,'" *Tim Ferriss Show* (blog), July 31, 2013, tim.blog/2013/07/31/why-and-how-creative-people-need-to-say-no.

4. Shannon L. Sibbald, Peter A. Singer, Ross Upshur, and Douglas K. Martin, "Priority Setting: What Constitutes Success? A Conceptual Framework for Successful Priority Setting," *BMC Health Services Research* 9 (2009): 43, https://doi.org/10.1186/1472-6963-9-43.

5. Thomas H. Davenport, *Thinking for a Living: How to Get Better Performances and Results from Knowledge Workers* (Boston: Harvard Business School Press, 2005), 155.

Chapter Seven: Master Delegation

1. The first three questions are adapted from Fortune Management's "Blueprint for Success." For more information, contact Fortune Management at fortunemgmt.com.

Chapter Nine: Don't Check Email, Process It

1. Emma Innes, "Is Your Inbox Making You Ill? Reading Work Emails Causes Your Blood Pressure and Heart Rate to Soar," *Daily Mail*, June 4, 2013, dailymail.co.uk/health/article-2335699/Is-inbox-making-ill-Reading-work-emails-causes-blood-pressure-heart-rate-soar.html.

Chapter Ten: Be Your Most Productive Self

1. Rasmus Hougaard and Jacqueline Carter, "How to Practice Mindfulness Throughout Your Work Day," *Harvard Business Review*, March 4, 2016, hbr.org/2016/03/how-to-practice-mindfulness-throughout-your-work-day.
2. Kimberly Schaufenbuel, "Bringing Mindfulness to the Workplace" (UNC Executive Development, UNC Kenan-Flagler Business School, 2014), kenan-flagler.unc.edu/~/media/Files/documents/executive-development/unc-white-paper-bringing-mindfulness-to-the-workplace_final.pdf.
3. Don Khouri, "The Mindset of Senior-Level Knowledge Workers when Evaluating Requests for Their Time" (PhD diss., Fielding Graduate University, 2016).
4. David Gelles, "The Mind Business," *Financial Times*, August 24, 2012, ft.com/content/d9cb7940-ebea-11e1-985a-00144feab49a.

Further Reading

Getting Things Done: The Art of Stress-Free Productivity, David Allen
Making It All Work: Winning at the Game of Work and Business of Life,
    David Allen
First Things First, Stephen R. Covey, A. Roger Merrill, and Rebecca R.
    Merrill
Mindset: Changing the Way You Think to Fulfil Your Potential, Carol
    Dweck
Organize Your Mind, Organize Your Life, Paul Hammerness and
    Margaret Moore
*The One Thing: The Surprisingly Simple Truth behind Extraordinary
    Results*, Garry Keller
*The Organized Mind: Thinking Straight in the Age of Information
    Overload*, Daniel Levitin
When: The Scientific Secrets of Perfect Timing, Daniel Pink

About the Author

ON KHOURI, PHD, is a speaker, author, and executive coach with a proven track record of coaching leaders and high-potential employees to attain maximum productivity, strengthen their communication and relationship skills, and motivate and inspire teams. He is an expert in personal productivity, organizational design, and building and leading high-performing, culturally diverse teams. He holds a PhD in human and organizational systems and a certificate in executive coaching.

Don is the managing director of Fortune Management Northeast, the country's leading and largest executive coaching firm for dentists. He served Fidelity Investments for 21 years in various leadership positions. As a vice president with responsibilities in software development, quality assurance, program management, and market data systems, Don has a track record of guiding highly complex, corporate-wide technology programs from inception to completion. His expertise also includes building high-performance international teams, with offices ranging from Boston to Bangalore and Dallas to Paris. He was an influential steering committee member of Fidelity Investments Technology's Mentoring Program, which paired over 500 technology associates interested in personal development with senior leaders.

Don previously served as organizational advisor at the Institute of Coaching at McLean Hospital, a Harvard Medical School Affiliate. In this role, he consulted with the Institute's directors on organization, was responsible for coordinating volunteers, and implemented a project management discipline. The Institute is building the scientific foundation for the practice of coaching.

Don's professional and academic credentials back up his broad and unique work experience. In addition to the PhD, he holds a BS degree in Management Information Systems and Quantitative Methods from Babson College, an MBA from Boston University focusing on organizational behavior, and an MA in Human Development from Fielding Graduate University. Don received the Graduate Certificate in Executive Coaching (GCEC) from the Massachusetts School of Professional Psychology. He is also a graduate of Legacy Learning Coach Training (the successor of FranklinCovey).

**Please stay connected with me online.
Here are several ways to connect:**

For book resources: whentosayyes.com

Author and speaker website: donkhouri.com

Twitter: @donkhouri

Facebook: Facebook.com/donkhouri

Instagram: @don.khouri

For dentists, check out my YouTube channel:
YouTube.com/user/YourDentalCoach

CPSIA information can be obtained
at www.ICGtesting.com
Printed in the USA
BVHW080036080921
616209BV00011B/337

9 781774 581391